The Trailblazer

Arizona to Africa and Back

To Margie, thank you for your labour of love, on the book Love your friend Sister Sharon

Sharon Ikerd

Dot Beams

Printed in the United States of America

First Printing, 2017

ISBN - 9781974185009

Kingdom Publisher
14121 Old Glen Highway.
Eagle River, AK 99577

Dedication

I dedicate this book to my wonderful children, Keith and Kelli, who have lived through many of the experiences. You are great trailblazers.

I give honor to the rest of my family - my lovely daughter-in-law, Elizabeth, my grandchildren, Mikey and his wife, Samantha (Sam), Jordan and his wife, Kristin, Benjamin, Aubrey, and my new twin great grandsons, Gunnar and little Mikey.

You are my greatest treasures and I love you.

Contents

Foreword

Brother Don Ikerd was one of the most humorous, loveable, brilliant, dedicated, out of the box missionaries that I have ever known. He was completely loyal and a true Christian. He was unique and very successful in his missionary work. His methods were often different and many didn't realize until later what he was doing.

Brother and Sister Ikerd did an amazing work for the Lord in Zambia in spite of the very great disappointments and frustrations they faced. They were not quitters and placed their trust in the Lord. Brother Ikerd's unusual sense of humor no doubt helped them through many difficult events in their lives.

In South Africa the Foreign Missions Division faced a serious challenge when all of the appointed missionaries working in South Africa decided to return to the homeland. At that time there was a fifteen man committee seeking to coordinate the activity of the four different churches in South Africa including the Whites, Coloreds, Indians, and Blacks, each division having its own superintendent, board, etc. This was all very frustrating and no doubt made it very difficult for the missionaries from North America.

How well I remember the lengthy prayerful discussion when the Foreign Missions Board was trying to find a missionary in Africa who could face the challenge of working with this fifteen man committee. Would this committee accept another missionary after great disappointment of all the other missionaries leaving? The South African committee indicated they did want missionaries.

The Foreign Missions Board felt that one missionary in Africa could fit into this unusual situation and that was Don Ikerd. We knew that Brother Ikerd would work with them as a friend with a spirit of humility.

I called Brother Ikerd and asked if he would be willing to consider leaving Zambia to go to South Africa. He wanted some time to pray about it. Before the close of the board meeting Brother Ikerd informed us that he and Sister Ikerd were willing to make this move if the church in South Africa would accept them.

Eventually I presented Brother Ikerd to the fifteen man committee. After hearing what he had to say, the committee told us they welcomed the Ikerds. Brother and Sister Ikerd showered love on the church in South Africa as fellow servants of Jesus Christ. They won their confidence. In time, Brother Ikerd was able to lead the church in South Africa to a unity never before experienced, where the church in all of South Africa had one superintendent and one committee.

One of my last experiences with Don Ikerd in South Africa was to observe him conducting a very important business meeting for the election of officers starting with the superintendent.

He asked the voting body if anyone among them would like to have this position. Three or four people raised their hands. Then they were told to cast their vote. For every position he gave the voters an opportunity to express their interest in having that office. Only then the vote was cast. The election went well. During the election of officers his cell phone rang. Sister Ikerd was calling. He stood in front talking to Sister Ikerd while the rest of us were waiting to continue the business. Everything was very informal, and the voting body seem very pleased with the way the business was conducted.

In dealing with the people of other languages and cultures, Don Ikerd had such a kind, friendly, manner. People seemed relaxed and happy. He had a wonderful way of putting people at ease. It is not a surprise that he was so loved everywhere he went.

> *Harry E. Scism*
> *Retired General Director of Global Missions*
> *United Pentecostal Church International*

Preface

I knew from the time my husband passed I would need to write about our life in missions. Even though I put it off for years, God often reminded me it needed to be done. Many times I sat at his desk and tried to come up with a title for the book.

While I was in Seychelles on an Associates in Mission (AIM) assignment in 2015, my daughter, Kelli, kept asking about selling her Dad's old trailblazer. During my four years on the AIM assignment to three Indian Ocean islands, the vehicle was getting older with many miles. It had been deteriorating as it sat in the hot Arizona sun for almost four years of no usage.

Kelli tried using the blazer every now and then during that time. The vehicle needed to be sold while we still could. I had put off selling it as my husband had loved that trailblazer. It was the last thing of his I had hung onto after his death.

One morning while in prayer, I started to cry. Kelli had just told me she had a buyer for her Dad's old automobile. She said it was rotting in the hot Arizona sun and it should be sold.

While in prayer, the Lord spoke to me and said, "It is okay to sell it. It's not the automobile that was the trailblazer; it was the man." At once I emailed Kelli to sell it.

My husband was a real trailblazer for the Lord. That was his life, his ministry, and his passion. I decided to entitle this book, "The Trailblazer", because that was him. The trailblazer put his heart and soul into twenty-eight years of missions.

Introduction

I want this book to get into the hands of every Christian to well remember what happened during South Africa's numerous adjustments when apartheid ended. The land started making many changes. This did not happen overnight. If this book had not been written, few would know what actually took place in the church concerning apartheid.

On the following pages you will read and feel the "heartbeat" of a man who blazed his way around Arizona, then across Africa. He started the foreign missions trail in Kenya, then it reached into Ethiopia, and Zambia (he pioneered the United Pentecostal Church work in this country). The trailblazer even trekked into Zaire.

The road led him from Zambia to South Africa where he was instrumental in bringing the church together, after being segregated for years by the apartheid system. You will read about his numerous trips to see and encourage pastors in many areas throughout the country. These trips were long and tiring. As the pioneer traveled, he planted seeds of tolerance, forgiveness, and love. The trailblazer was able to see walls come down little by little. There were many changes as the churches of South Africa moved forward together.

The Lord had promised to give my husband and I instructions and guide us on the many trials that laid ahead. "I will instruct thee and teach thee in the way which thou shalt go. I will guide thee with my eye" (Psalms 32:8). God daily watched over us with His eye. He taught us to listen to His voice as He is the best GPS system in the world.

My husband went on to his reward eight years ago. Only now can I write the words of the many stories he was fond of telling. The years in Africa changed our lives. May the reading of this book change your life.

Trails Ablaze

After asking what they would name their son, the delivery doctor took a pen and wrote the baby's full name on the bedroom wall. Donald Eugene Ikerd was born at home in Visalia, California on August 30, 1935 to John Elbert and Lee Etta Ikerd.

The Lord had his hand on Don from birth. God called him like he called Jeremiah. "Before I formed thee in the belly, I knew thee: and before thou camest forth out of the womb I sanctified thee, and I ordained thee a prophet unto the nations" (Jeremiah 1:5).

One day God moved upon Mom Ikerd to pray while making a vow to God, "I will dedicate the first one of my children to come through the door to you," assuming it would be her oldest. As she continued to pray for several minutes, her second son, Donald Eugene, came through the door. He just stood there as if waiting on something. Going up to him, she laid her hands on his head and prayed that God would use him for His glory, never dreaming that someday he would become a preacher, pastor, and missionary to Africa.

Don received the Holy Ghost on January 11, 1953. There were three men that would make an impact on his life. All had been missionaries to Africa. He would become a real trailblazer for the truth.

After his father's death, Don joined the Air Force in 1957 to see the world while his older brother, Ray, had joined the Navy. Don went to boot camp and received his orders to go to Vincent Air Force Base in Yuma, Arizona. What a disappointment since he was not going to travel and see the world as he had been promised by the recruiter. Yuma is a small town in the middle of the desert and known as the hottest place in the nation.

Don and I were married on January 27, 1959 in Yuma. Six months later the Vincent Air Force Base was phased out and Don received his orders to Tampa, Florida. The trailblazer and I made our way from Yuma to Tampa while traveling in an old 1952 Studebaker. Many experiences in the Tampa church prepared us for the trails ahead. After working in home missions fourteen years, God had been dealing with Don for over a year about foreign missions, specifically Africa.

The trailblazer had a dream where God showed him a missionary in Africa that would go into the bush but would not come out. God told him to go to that country as they would need his help. It was not long until we heard Brother Cupples, missionary to Kenya, had been killed in an auto accident. My husband felt that Kenya was where he was to go. After much prayer and fasting, Don requested a foreign missions application.

The Mailman

The foreign missions application came quickly. Don filled out the application and was ready to send it in. I decided that if he wanted to go to Africa, I really needed to talk to the Lord since I had mixed emotions because we had just moved into our first new home.

Walking to the side door of the sanctuary, I opened it and knelt at the first pew. I told God, "If you can speak to my husband about going to Africa, you can speak to me." After much prayer, I was a changed person upon leaving the sanctuary. I came out with a burden and a love for Africa which is still with me today.

During the same time I was in prayer, Don was having his own talk with God. He felt the Lord let him know that he was called to Kenya, East Africa. But, he wanted to be sure. That morning he prayed and told the Lord, "If you want us to go to Kenya, send a magazine about the country in the mail today by 10:00 am." If it does not come by that time, I'll know it's not Your will."

As he continued in prayer, the mailman came just before the normal time. When my husband went to the mail box, he found a small magazine wrapped in brown paper. Tearing off the paper, there in big letters on a magazine cover was "Revival in Kenya East Africa". The entire magazine featured Kenya. Don looked at the brown paper to see who had sent it. It had been mailed from Nairobi, Kenya almost a month before. As he examined the envelope, he realized the magazine had been delivered to the wrong address - but God had sent it to the right address at the right time. The intended recipient of the magazine was happy for us to keep it. We kept the little magazine for years.

The confirmation received from God regarding Kenya prompted Don to mail the foreign missions application. This was in 1972. A few weeks later we received notice from the Foreign Missions Department to wait to meet the Foreign Missions Board the next year at general conference.

The Board Meeting

Sometime in August of the next year, our foreign missions application papers were returned to us. Brother Box, the Secretary/Treasurer for the Foreign Missions Department (FMD), asked my husband to pray about choosing another country. The reason was several had applied for Kenya ahead of us, and he felt there were other countries in need of a missionary. Brother Box mentioned several countries and my husband chose the country of Malawi. After we discussed his letter, my husband told me, "It's okay. We will receive our appointment for Kenya."

The trailblazer and I made our way to Salt Lake City, trusting the Lord to take care of everything. Sister Freeman went with us to the hotel Tuesday morning, the location of the Foreign Missions Board meeting. As her husband was a board member, she asked me to take some vitamins to him. Sister Freeman scooped a large handful into my hand because she did not have a package for them. I was a nervous wreck. The board was full of men who were very frightening to me. My hand was running with perspiration. Looking down a few minutes later, my fist had a rainbow of colors running out of it. There seemed no time or place to give them to Brother Freeman.

At last, I walked over to Brother Freeman who was sitting at the other end of the table, and placed the vitamins in front of him. The room exploded in laughter. Everyone could see the vitamins were beyond taking. Thank God that broke the ice.

My husband was asked several questions before we left the meeting. Brother Freeman requested the board to have special prayer. Gathering around us, they asked God to have His way in our lives.

Wednesday we called home to tell our church and family that we were not appointed. Thursday morning Sister Freeman came to the Home Missions booth where we were working and said, "Come quickly. The board is waiting to talk to you again."

Rushing to the boardroom, once again they asked us questions. This time the questions were about Kenya and not Malawi. My husband was asked if he would be willing to work under Brother John Harris, a younger man, the superintendent of Kenya. He told them age did not matter.

Brother T. F. Tenney, Foreign Missions Director, gestured with his long pointer to Kenya on a wall map and asked Don if he would agree to accept the responsibility of the Bible school that was to be built. Happily he agreed.

During the beginning of the evening service, we watched Brother Box, one of the board members, leave the platform and work his way through the bleachers towards us. When he came as close as he could, he cupped his hands to his mouth and shouted, "Brother Ikerd, get your suitcases packed. You received your appointment to Kenya."

God had answered our prayers again and we rejoiced. Immediately we left the service to phone my sister, Fern, and her husband. Since they were taking care of Keith and Kelli, we wanted them to bring our children for Sunday's Foreign Mission service. Quickly they packed and drove to the conference for the commissioning service on October 4, 1973.

Headquarters requested us to attend the first School of Missions in Columbus, Ohio where daily classes were taught by missionaries and Foreign Missions Board members. Classes were followed by wonderful evangelistic evening meetings. We realized how valuable the teachings would be when we arrived on the foreign field.

Once our deputation was finished, we drove back to Prescott to visit a couple of weeks with my family.

Two Black Eyes

Now we were ready to rent a U-Haul truck and start the long trail across the western states to the New Orleans shipping dock. A friend of my sister, Sister Margie Hoyle, came to help in the Prescott church during our last weeks. She knocked on doors, gave out tracts, and held Bible studies. What a blessing she was to help us get the drums packed, which were then spot-welded, and loaded in the U-Haul truck.

Once we said goodbye to our family, we drove to Pampa, Texas to visit more family. Arriving in Reed, Oklahoma on Saturday afternoon, where my grandmother, Sister Oma Ellis, was pastoring, we stayed over for their Sunday morning service. Due to our timeline to get our things to the dock, we left after the service.

Late that Sunday afternoon on a two-lane road in Oklahoma, two little old ladies stopped their car in front of ours. Don stopped but a brand new big-rig truck behind us could not stop. The truck hit us, pushing us into their car, sending it across the highway into a ditch. Thank the Lord there was no one coming in the opposite direction.

Kelli had been sitting on my lap in our big U-Haul truck cab. Upon impact, her head hit my face breaking my nose. Both of us were covered with blood. The young truck driver came up to my window and said, "I tried to stop but was unable to."

Since the accident happened in the countryside, only a few cars came by. One car took Kelli and I to the nearest hospital. The nurses could not believe she was unhurt because she was covered in blood as well as her doll, Susie. Because no doctor was on duty at this country hospital, one was called in. X-rays of my nose were needed but Kelli clung to me and refused to let go. Finally, the nurses talked her into going with one of them to wash her and the doll. Kelli talked to the nurse and doctor while I had the x-ray and told them we were new missionaries headed to Kenya, East Africa.

Other than a crushed nose, I was fine. The doctor had a unique way of setting my nose but not a very sanitary one, and probably not considered a professional method today. Slipping a pen out of his shirt pocket, he used the end of it to pull my nose straight. After that he packed my nose full of gauze and more gauze, I had no idea that a nose could hold that much.

While Kelli and I were at the hospital, my husband and Keith stayed with our rental truck. After the police investigated the accident and made their report, Don set out to find us by driving to a couple of nearby small towns, finally locating us.

Back on the road again. Kelli and I could not go into a restaurant since we were still in our blood-soaked clothes. Eventually we found an old drive-in restaurant where they delivered food on a tray. The car hop looked shocked when she saw us. I explained we had been in an accident but were okay. Late that night we found a motel. Because none of us could get to our night clothes which were still in the smashed truck, we slept as we were.

Finally we were able to get another truck, pick up clean clothes, load our items, and get back on the road. Early the next morning, we arrived in New Orleans and found a motel close to the dock. After sleeping a few hours, the children and I stayed at the motel while my husband delivered our shipment to the dock.

Airborne At Last

The next morning we were scheduled to fly from New Orleans to New York. Since I had never flown before, I had no desire and had told my husband, "I will never fly."

God had a different idea. That morning at the New Orleans airport I explained to the clerk we were taking things to our friends in Kenya, Africa. She allowed us to fly but told us, "They will never let you take all of that on the overseas flight because you are completely overloaded."

Don instructed Keith and I to check in with our luggage. When the lady weighted our suitcases, she said, "You will need to pay over three hundred dollars for the extra weight." We did not have the money nor a credit card.

Although we arrived early at the airport, our flight would not leave until that evening. Moving to the side of the counter, I began sorting our things and setting them on the floor while quietly crying not wanting to leave any of the items behind.

Don decided to take the extra weight in one of the suitcases to the Greyhound bus and send it to my mother. I repacked while my husband and I silently prayed for guidance. The airport was almost empty. No one was around except an African man in an airport uniform. Among our packed items were many things for the Harris family - two pairs of blue jeans for each boy, lunch boxes, and other items Sister Harris had ordered from the states. Included was a gift for each Harris child. Even though we had never met the Harrises, we knew they would become like family.

At last, the uniformed man walked over to me and said, "Mam, where do you want that suitcase to go?"

I replied, "Nairobi, Kenya."

He said, "That is your plane," as he pointed to the window where we could see the big Pan Am plane.

The gentleman said, "Give me the suitcase and I will put it in the plane for you."

I looked at Don and he said, "Okay."

The man picked up the suitcase and stated, "I will wave at you when I get it loaded."

As we watched him through the plate glass window, he walked up to the plane door where cargo had been loaded, opened it, and put the suitcase inside. Afterwards, the man walked to the back of the plane and waved to us; we were to never see him again.

It was a few years later when I again boarded a Pan Am plane. Looking down from my window, I realized the man who had helped us load the suitcase on our first plane to Kenya had to have been nine feet tall to open that door. God had done a miracle for us.

When we boarded the plane that evening, we still had too much hand luggage. Kelli was carrying two large dolls, one for Jodi Harris and one for her. Keith had balls and mitt and other things for the Harris boys.

The stewardess insisted we could not take all our carry-on pieces. I explained the items were for a missionary family's children in Kenya. At last she said, "You can take what you can get under the seats in front of you, which we did by stuffing all under the seats. Finally we were buckled up and ready to fly. Thankfully, the seat next to Kelli was empty; she was able to put both the big dolls in the seat.

The old Pan Am flight stopped in most West Africa countries. Having no flying experience, I did not know what to expect. The flight was choppy and very rough - like riding a donkey. Seat belts had to be fastened most of the long flight.

Bouncing roughly along the Liberia air strip and seeing cows outside our window, I thought we missed the runway. When we landed in Nigeria, soldiers boarded the plane looking at every passenger and checking all passports. During this time, the airplane motor was turned off leaving us with no air conditioning. It was very hot in the plane. Keith and Kelli were tired of sitting and decided to get some fresh air while looking at all the strange sights out the open door. The country had experienced another coup which held up our plane a long time. The soldiers told our children to go back inside and return to their seats.

Finally, the soldiers made one more trip through the plane and gave us permission to depart. There was a great sigh of relief from everyone knowing we were on our way again. Next stop Kenya.

Wonders of a New Land

Arriving late at night in Kenya, the land of our calling, Brother John Harris and his family met us at the airport. They brought two cars to the airport. One was their family car and the other was our new Peugeot 504. The vehicle had been purchased for us so we would have transportation. The first piece of our luggage to get off the plane was the suitcase the man had graciously put on the plane for us free of charge. The Lord kept His hand on us and all our things arrived safely.

Our arrival on August 30, 1974 was a very special day - Don's 39th birthday. The Harrises took us home with them where Sister Harris had prepared a meal.

When we arrived in Kenya, I still had two black eyes from the U-Haul accident. While on deputation, Brother Box called to let us know Brother Harris had found land in Kenya with an old house eliminating our need to find one. It was located off the Waiyaki Way, which was the main road to western Kenya and to Uganda. If we agreed, they would purchase it for the Bible school and headquarters' church. Since our rent would pay for the property, we agreed sight unseen.

In the morning we saw all the wonders and beauty of Nairobi Kenya, the capital city. It is set about 6,000 feet above sea level and is a very beautiful place with lavender-blooming Jackaranda trees and African flame trees with flamboyant dark red-orange flowers. What a lovely sight met our eyes after living in Arizona.

Kenya is a land of many tribes and different tribal languages. Swahili and English are the two official languages. At first sight, we loved our new land and, most of all, the people. Kenyans were friendly, always smiling, and were very open to the message of truth. We were thrilled with what God was doing in the churches throughout the country. The Harris family made us very welcome; we enjoyed the food and fellowship while staying with them a couple of weeks until our house was ready.

The first day we looked at the property to see what needed to be done to move into the house. The large old home, which had been empty for some time, was only a short distance from the Harrises. At first sight, it needed a lot of tender loving care. Steps were broken, the house needed paint, and the kitchen was in need of a lot of work. There were no cupboards, shelves, sink or draining board. A large, shallow country sink was sitting in the corner. After cleaning and painting, we moved into the house while the kitchen and bathroom were being remodeled. In spite of all the flaws, we loved the old house and share many fond memories of our years there.

The Harris family of six was a great blessing to us. They had four children, David, Robert, Jonathan, and Jodi, who became good friends to our children and remain friends to this day. They helped us in every way possible. Brother Harris taught my husband to drive on the opposite side of the road; they had a few challenges. One day during a driving lesson, Don drove around the roundabout in the wrong direction. Brother Harris almost jumped out of the car.

The first Sunday we attended church across town in a rented Young Men's Christian Association (YMCA) room. A baptismal service was held that day and Brother Harris had asked my husband to do the baptism. A young man named Steven was baptized who later came to the Bible school and became an interpreter for my husband.

Sister Harris took me to the nice places to grocery shop. I learned to shop for meat at the meat market. Vegetables and fruits were at the green grocer. All milk, boxed in the shape of a triangle, was sitting unrefrigerated on the floor in the main grocer. Sugar came in little brown bags. There were no brands. If the grocer had an item you had better get it. Hamburger was called minced meat. There were no supplies for the children's lunch boxes. Whatever you put in them, you made it. If you wanted cookies, cake, potato chips or crackers you made it. Crackers we made did not taste like American crackers but we learned to eat them.

Arrival in Kenya was just in time for the kids' school to start, as well as we started classes at the Swahili school, where Sister Harris joined us.

Language school and trying to learn the Kenyan customs filled our first months. The men did a lot of traveling. Brother Harris helped my husband find his way to our churches around Kenya. There was much to be done before the Harris family left on deputation to raise their financial support.

Brother Harris took Don to Ethiopia since my husband would need to visit there while he was on leave. On one of these trips, they brought home many boxes of cold cereal from the American Commissary - Rice Crispy, Corn Pops, Cheerio, and others. What great excitement we experienced when we all sat down to enjoy the American cereals. Each cereal had be to tried. When we were about finished, one of the kids looked on a box to find the expiration date. Definitely expired and everyone had a good laugh.

Kenyans had yet to perfect cereal. Their only cereal was corn flakes which was thick with corn kernels in them and hard on your teeth.

While we were adjusting to Kenya, Brother Harris asked our family to go with them to the Amboseli National Game Park for our first long school break. The decision was made to leave at the end of the week. Part of the way was paved and part was dirt roads. The dirt road was about 100 kilometers long and very difficult to drive. The trailblazer was happy on paved or dirt roads.

About halfway to the park, we stopped at a village to rest. There were many Maasai, the most primitive tribe in the country. Our children saw an old Maasai man with a 26-ounce Blue Band margarine can in one of his earlobes (about the size of a Morton salt box). It hung almost to his shoulder. The main article of clothing worn by this tribe was a red blanket with no undergarments. Young warriors wore loin cloths. This was all new and eye-popping to the Ikerd family.

The Amboseli National Game Park lays on the border of Tanzania and Kenya. Mount Kilimanjaro can be seen throughout the park with snow on top year round. We stayed in a little rondavel (hut) made of cement with a grass thatched roof for about $5 a night, and had a great time. Sheets, towels, and mosquito netting were provided for each bed.

This trip was our first experience with mosquito nets. What a blessing they were. The thatched roofs kept the place cooler. How happy we were the first morning when we awoke to wildlife by our hut. It was fascinating to see them in their natural habitat. My husband soon learned to get up early for a morning drive to the water ponds where there was a variety of animals. Later in the morning, we returned to our little huts where we cooked our breakfast and rested until late afternoon. Then we drove to another watering hole. The children loved to watch the hippos swim in the water. Often they saw crocodiles sunning on the rocks.

An unforgettable experience happened one day. The two cars we were traveling in came around a corner only to see a very large dead elephant in the road. A Maasai warrior had killed it moments before and had run off when he heard our vehicles. His poisoned spear was still stuck in its side because he would hope to return and cut off the very expensive tusks, a poacher's prize. Even though lying on its side, the giant elephant was taller than our cars. One car stayed with the elephant to discourage the poacher from returning while the other car went for a game warden.

Our return trip was hot and tiring but we all enjoyed the park very much. This park became one of our favorite places to visit since the wild life was plentiful.

First Christmas in Kenya

Christmas in Kenya was approaching. There were no turkeys so we roasted large chickens. Shopping was limited so toys and sports equipment could not be found. I had already sent a concerned letter to my sister and mother so they could airmail something for the children, praying their packages would arrive on time as mail was not always dependable.

The Christmas package arrived on time, thank the Lord. The box from my sister and her husband made Keith and Kelli's holiday a very special one. Included for Kelli was a pink plastic tea set from my sister and pink cookie cutters from my mother. Keith received a battery-operated car and bike pump, which he needed for his bike and airing his soccer ball. Since there were no kind of battery-operated cars in Kenya, it was a very special gift.

Keith asked his Dad if he would take him over to see David and Robert, the older Harris boys, because he wanted to show off his new race car. Just before they left, Brother Harris arrived with Jodi, the Harris' daughter. Soon after their arrival, Kelli and Jodi had their first tea party. Many times later, when the girls had tea parties, they were teased by Keith and the three Harris boys.

29

Keith asked if he could walk to the Harris' home to share his Christmas gifts. Once his Dad approved, he packed a bag. Looking into his bag, I saw the new race car, tire pump and new soccer ball. The battery-operated car was worn out in one day, but the boys enjoyed every minute. Our family celebrated Christmas at the Harris' home with a wonderful holiday and a delicious home-cooked dinner.

The drums shipped to Kenya filled with our items finally arrived. During our long wait, Kelli often cried for her favorite stuffed monkey, which was in one of the drums. I did not realize how long our things would be in coming. Kelli was so glad to see the drums she hugged each of the twenty-one saying, "You made it! You made it!" How thrilled she was, at long last to be reunited with her monkey.

When we began opening the drums, two were empty. Another was half empty and filled with items that were not ours. Don's typewriter was missing and other important office supplies. There was nothing we could do about it.

A missionary retreat was scheduled in a hotel in Pretoria, South Africa. Don booked our flight with the Harrises. All were looking forward to the retreat because it would be the first time the Ikerd family met all of the African region missionaries.

Brother and Sister Brian Orffer were in charge of the children's activities during the retreat and did a great job. During the day, the men had many games of chess. The ladies had hours of talking and laughing together. It was a wonderful time of fellowship. Our evenings were filled with uplifting services.

Kelli celebrated her eighth birthday while we were there. Sister Orffer baked her a special cake with a Barbie-like doll coming out of the middle. How we laughed when the doll was removed to cut the cake and realized the doll's shoes were missing. Carefully, we cut the cake and found the little shoes. Kelli was able to share her cake with all the missionary children.

Many times while we were at the hotel, the intercom came on to make announcements in Afrikaans. The announcement ended with the phrase, "baie dankie." Kelli said to her dad, "Daddy, why do they tell us we need to buy a donkey?" Her Dad laughed and explained it meant thank you very much in their language.

Brotherly Instruction

One morning I looked out the window to see a strange sight. Keith, our 12 year old, was teaching his eight-year-old sister how to carry a bucket on her head. African girls learned at an early age to carry water or heavy loads this way.

Kelli had a large bucket on her head. Keith put some big rocks in it. Her head wobbled as she tried to walk. When she dropped some of the rocks, Keith picked them up and put them back in the bucket. He came up with this lesson all on his own. Every time Kelli managed to make it around our circular driveway without spilling the rocks two or three times, Keith put in another large rock. Her load got heavier and heavier but he was a good teacher. Kelli learned to carry water on her head just like the other girls. A few years later, she was able to put this into practice.

Rookie Missionaries

When it was time for the Harris family to leave for the states, we had a farewell service for them. It was hard to see them leave.

Now we were rookie missionaries left on our own in Kenya. Many experiences lay ahead during the next 12 months as our family adjusted to a new culture and customs. The Harris family had only been gone a few days when a friend of theirs called Don and told him about a special entrance fee for Kenyan residents at the new game park, Maasai Mara Game Reserve. Our work permit qualified us for residency and my husband decided to take us. The road to the park was a very long dirt road, like a washboard. We were blessed to witness the annual wildebeest migration with thousands of them as far as you could see. It is rated as one of the world's most spectacular natural events with over one million wildebeests each year. From a distance, they appeared as small as ticks. Migration was never at the same time each year because it depended on the rain. Because the wildebeests were everywhere, we had to inch our car between them.

On our way out of the park we saw an old male lion. Our windows were rolled down since we had no air conditioning. Don was taking it easy on the dirt road because the dust was very bad. His eyes were on the rough road and did not see the lion. Kelli shouted, "Daddy, look at the lion!" The lion was about four feet from the car. My husband put his foot on the gas pedal and we got out of there.

Chicky, Chicky

After returning home from the Maasai Mara Game Reserve, the decision was made to travel to Western Kenya for services and make it a family affair. On our way, we stopped at the Kericho Tea Hotel and had a platter of sandwiches and tea while watching the workers harvest the tea. When we arrived in Kisumu, we stayed in a little old African hotel called, "The Talk of the Town", which it was. After the services each day, we drove back to our hotel trying to get back before dark.

Chicken was what we always ordered at the hotel as we knew it was fresh and safe. An order for chicken was always placed when you arrived because it would take over an hour before it was ready to eat. Keith and Kelli loved to go upstairs and look down in the yard where they could see someone chase a chicken around the yard, catch it, kill it, and dress it. The hotel usually had good cooks. We enjoyed it very much when it finally made it to our table.

Following our services, the Kenyan people always gave us a love offering to take home. A large stalk of bananas was a favorite, as well as sweet potatoes and two chickens. Don always kept the hens but butchered the roosters, since having more than one was a problem. What a blessing these were to our family.

Bag Lady

The weather was getting warmer and Christmas wasn't too far off. I decided to send the family something special from Kenya.

There was an excellent little Indian corner curio shop downtown that had some great carvings. Kelli insisted that she come along with me. Once inside the shop, she decided it was too hot and stuffy so asked if she could sit on a stool just outside the front door. The shopkeeper said, "It will be no problem. I will keep an eye on her."

The stool was rather tall, but with a bit of effort Kelli managed to climb up and get herself seated all the while getting her dress stuck on the back of the stool.

I was busy inside, down on my knees going through wooden animal-carved napkin rings trying to match up pairs when a blood-curdling scream came from the front door.

Jumping up, I looked and saw Kelli and the stool toppling over as the city bag lady hurried off down the street. The bag lady wasn't right in her mind. Wearing black plastic trash bags that didn't cover her up very well, she lived on the street and ate scraps from the trash. Even though harmless, she was just a little crazy.

The shopkeeper and I hurried over to see what had happened. There stood Kelli, gagging and crying. As the bag lady wondered on down the street she kept saying, "I just wanted to kiss the baby white girl."

Kelli was mortified and said, "She didn't kiss me, Mama, she licked me from my chin to my forehead!" Once we knew everything was fine, all of us had a good laugh, with the exception of Kelli, of course.

Unusual Love Offering

My husband set up a ministers' seminar in the western area of Kenya. A special project was arranged for wives and lady leaders to make neck ties to sell and raise funds for our national leader to attend the World Conference in the coming year.

There was great excitement in our sewing class. How I missed Sister Harris, as she was handy with her hands and very talented in making things. One of my husband's ties was taken apart and a pattern made from it. The little hut we used for sewing was dark, making seeing difficult. Keith and Kelli were kept very busy threading everyone's needles. All of the ties were hand sewn by each woman. The ladies were very proud of their accomplishments as each was able to show off her handiwork.

Late in the evening, my husband taught on giving. One of the sisters asked me, "How do you give when you do not have any shillings?"

I answered, "You can give what you raise or what you take to market to sell."

On the last day, we were given a very unusual offering - a large African basket. The ladies placed the basket on the floor while dancing and singing around it. The bottom was filled with two to three inches of dry beans. As they danced, each lady placed an egg on the beans until the beans were covered. Another row of beans was then poured into the basket followed by each lady placing another egg. Rows of beans and eggs continued until the basket was completely filled. What a wonderful gift - 107 eggs - their love offering to us.

Not one egg broke on the six-hour trip home. The evening's teaching brought forth results; they were blessed in their giving.

Elephant Breakfast

The King family from San Antonio, Texas came to visit accompanied by Sister Bobbye Wendell. Brother King was to be our special speaker for our upcoming meeting. In addition, there was to be a baptismal service and a baby dedication. Over thirty were baptized. The baby dedication was a new experience for Brother King. He never forgot it since almost all of the babies decided to have their lunch at that time.

Following the special meeting, we decided to take our guests with our children to the Amboseli National Park. This park is Kenya's second most popular national park. It has the best reputation for getting up close to free-range elephants.

All the car windows were down in our little 504 Peugeot the day we traveled. My husband tried to take it easy on the old rough dirt road. Since Brother King had jetlag, he fell asleep in the front seat. Sister King, Sister Wendell, Keith, and I rode in the back seat. Thankfully, Kelli could still squeeze into the space between the two front seats. When the kids saw different animals, they would awaken Brother King and he would grab the camera hanging on his neck and ask, "Where? Where?" The children pointed and he started snapping pictures.

When we arrived at the rondavels for the night, Brother King laid his camera case on the hood of our car. Before he knew it, a monkey jumped up on the car, snatched it, and climbed a nearby tree. Brother King was most upset so their Dad had Keith and Kelli take bananas to try to coax the guilty monkey down. The monkey finally let go of the camera case to take a banana.

Kelli decided to stay in Sister Wendell's rondavel. All rondavels were roofed with grass. In the early morning hours, an elephant decided to eat part of their roof for its breakfast. Kelli was afraid and started crying, wanting to come to our rondavel. Her Dad shouted to her she had to stay and not come to our hut since the elephant would attack her. Sister Wendell had to hold her while she continued to cry and scream. At long last, the elephant finished his breakfast, leaving most of the roof, and turned towards our car parked nearby. When he left, we could no longer see him. Suddenly, we heard a loud banging, stomping, and metal crushing. Don knew our car was finished and he wondered how he would tell Brother Paul Box. When my husband checked on our car the next morning, there was no damage. Nearby lay several smashed metal trash cans. Thankfully, our car was all right.

Lots of animals were seen on that trip and we had a grand time, returning to Nairobi in time for the start of the children's school. The Kings and Sister Wendell stayed and visited a few more days. Before they left, Don took them to see the flamingoes at Lake Nakuru, which was always a lovely sight. Their visit blessed our lives.

13th Birthday

Don was a great family man and father, often taking time for his children. Keith's thirteenth birthday was coming up and his Dad wanted to do something special so he planned a camping and fishing trip to his favorite place, Lake Naivasha. Our good friends, the Johnsons, who were like an aunt and uncle to our children, were invited.

Keith and Kelli had a great time packing for this trip. Thankfully, my husband thought to take Sukie, the Harris' old dog, with us for a guard around the camp. Sukie was older but more reliable to stay at the camp than our two young dogs. Arriving in late afternoon, Keith helped his Dad find a good camp spot and put up our four-man tent. Then they helped Brother Johnson with his tent.

The fellows set off in the rental boat. While they were gone, Kelli kept busy catching little minnows in her can. She also helped us get ready to cook on the open fire. When they returned, we had fish for dinner. It was wonderful to sit around the campfire enjoying the fresh fish and fellowship until late in the evening.

Early the next day the fellows set off to try their hand at fishing again. The fishermen came back at lunch time bringing their prized catch with them. There was enough fish for lunch and dinner. Lake Naivasha was a great place to fish and they easily brought back plenty to cook.

Fresh air and plenty of sun made everyone tired so all turned in early. About midnight, we were awakened by Sukie as she made a lap around the tent barking at my husband's cot. Don stepped out the tent door and saw Brother Johnson with his flashlight. Soon they realized why Sukie was barking. Safari ants had surrounded our tent. What a job the men had killing them and by now, everyone was awake. It took a couple of hours to finish their task. Finally, we all returned to our cots to get some sleep before morning.

What a lovely campfire breakfast we had that morning - bacon, eggs, cowboy coffee, and French toast (Keith's favorite) cooked on the open fire.

Keith, his Dad, and Brother Johnson set off for their last fishing trip before returning home. Kelli kept busy catching minnows to entertain herself while Sister Johnson and I had another cup of coffee and read a book.

Keith had a wonderful thirteenth birthday and everyone was sorry to end the camping trip.

Bull That Came to Church

Almost every Saturday Don had special meetings teaching pastors. On one of these Saturdays, Kelli, Keith, and I traveled with their Dad so they could play with the children who were there. Someone gave Kelli a large piece of sugar cane. While she was enjoying it, a young bull kept butting her trying to take it from her. Kelli finally had enough and hit him on the nose. This made him very angry and he started after her.

When she ran, the bull was right behind her. She made one lap around the church while screaming at the top of her lungs, "Daddy! Daddy!"

During her next lap, she ran through the front door opening, right down the middle aisle, and out the side door. The young bull was right on her heels when her Dad started after the bull. All the pastors joined in the chase. How I wished I had had a video camera that day. Of course, Kelli would not drop her sugar cane for the bull. At last the men caught the young bull while Kelli finally stopped running and finished her sugar cane.

Adventure in Ethiopia

Don planned to attend an Easter conference in Ethiopia, which was held the week after our Easter. The Foreign Missions Department gave me permission to attend with him. It was my only trip to this country yet I never forgot it even though it has been over 41 years. Ethiopia's calendar had been stopped for five years while their emperor, Haile Selassie, was in exile. This was the first time we celebrated Easter twice in one year.

The Johnsons volunteered to take care of our children while we were gone. Keith and Kelli were very fond of them. We knew they would be in good hands.

Ethiopia had a petrol shortage. The brothers felt it was not wise to take a car all the way to Awasa, our destination, because it was several hours away. The only alternative was to ride the old, slow country bus which had a lot to be desired. Don and Brother Harris had ridden them before but this was my first time.

My husband told me I could stay in Addis Ababa with some of the sisters if I did not want to travel on the old bus, but I felt I should go with him.

Ethiopia was still experiencing much political unrest. Prompted by the Spirit, I wrote down the Johnson's phone number and our children's names since we were going into a war zone. That evening, we had dinner at a little Chinese restaurant belonging to a friend of Brother Harris, whom he had met while living in Ethiopia. I told Brother Harris' friend, "If anything happens to us, please call our friends and tell them to send our children to the states."

A brother in the church picked us up at our hotel and took us to the bus stop. The bus was full even though we arrived early. The driver went through the aisle putting up little pop-up seats, now making the bus wall-to-wall people. There was no way to stand or move. Twelve or more preachers were going with us and the wife of the national leader, the only lady besides myself. Two white people traveling on the bus created a lot of comments among the passengers.

The bus driver made a stop for the toilets when we had been traveling for some time. Someone in our group bought food for us. An armed soldier appeared while we waited our turn to leave the bus. After coming onboard, he yelled at us. When he saw my husband's Bible, he picked it up and threw it on the floor. No one said a word. At last we were allowed to get off the bus.

Upon returning to the bus, the armed soldier was standing in the doorway staring at us. When I looked around, the brothers had seated the wife of the national leader next to me and my husband. The rest of our group surrounded us. Quietly and earnestly we prayed trusting the Lord to protect us. Because my husband and I were in Ethiopia on a tourist visa, we did not have permission to hold services. A few years before, the government had closed all Pentecostal churches and had expelled the missionaries. Religious freedom was repressed and the church went underground.

When we arrived at the next large village, the soldier got off the bus. What a relief. I am sure he knew who we were and why we were there. After another couple of stops, we arrived at our destination.

At the final bus stop, we were met and taken to a little hotel similar to a bed and breakfast where we were able to bathe and rest a few minutes. That evening we went to the church service by donkey cart. The place was packed with people waiting for us to arrive. Tree branches were used to camouflage the outside of the building. People were told to keep silent and not worship out loud because church services were not being held in the open. Yet, Pentecostals cannot be quiet.

The first night, they did pretty good but by the second night, they were worshipping out loud when suddenly an armed soldier kicked in the door. He stood there a long time but people kept worshipping and Don continued preaching. After what seemed like a long time, the soldier turned and walked away. By the next night, we heard guns firing in the distance. For safety, the brothers felt we should leave the area and return to Addis Ababa, which we agreed.

God Goes First Class

Returning to Addis Ababa from Awasa by bus, we had only traveled a couple of hours when it ran out of petrol in the middle of nowhere. The bus driver told everyone to get off the bus and stand next to it. The national Ethiopian leader begged the driver to let us stay on the bus, but he would not allow it. There was no place to hide two white people. Car after car came by. Some stopped to give others a ride but no one wanted to take two white people to Addis Ababa through the road blocks.

The national leader flagged down a white Mercedes Benz and the driver agreed to take us. He put Don and I along with his wife in the back seat and off we went.

Don tried to talk to the driver, but the man did not respond. Thinking he did not know English, he asked the sister to talk to the man but she got no response making us unsure if we were traveling with a government man or someone from the opposition party.

Coming to our first roadblock, we knew it was not safe for us to be with the wrong political party. The driver got in line for the checkpoint. Soldiers had everyone ahead of us get out of their cars. Slowly we moved forward. Spikes were not down but there were armed soldiers on each side of the road stopping cars. When it was our time at the head of the roadblock, our driver drove through not stopping. Don looked back fearing soldiers would shoot, but nothing happened. Since I was sitting in the middle of the back seat and could see the front seat, I noticed the driver was holding a snub-nosed machine gun in his lap.

As we traveled on our way, there were more roadblocks. When we came to another checkpoint, soldiers were searching each car. Yet again, they did not stop us as our driver drove through the roadblock with no trouble.

There were no more cars ahead of us. Apparently, they had turned off somewhere along the way. At a new roadblock, two guards stood talking to each other. Again, we drove between them and continued on our way with no problem. Our mysterious driver drove us near the front of our hotel which was located a block off the road. Once he stopped the car, the driver said nothing. We assumed we were to get out. My husband thanked him and tried to offer money but he gave no response. The man drove off leaving us by the road.

We would never know if he was an angel sent by God or not. But one thing we knew for sure, he was our angel bringing us out of a war zone, through three road blocks traveling many kilometers, and delivering us safe and sound. Our God is mighty. He is the same yesterday, today, and forever. "The angel of the Lord encampeth round about them that fear Him, and delivereth them" (Psalms 34:7).

That night my husband and I stood on our hotel balcony praising the Lord for His mighty delivering power. We prayed God would send missionaries to that country. The next day we returned to Nairobi.

Raised from the Dead

Don had been teaching a Bible study in a new area of the city for some time. At one Bible study, he taught about the lady who had been raised from the dead (John 4:1-37). Quite a discussion took place in that class and the students wanted to know if the Lord could or would do such things today. He shared with them miraculous testimonies from Ethiopia and other places where there had been reports of people being raised from the dead.

A few days later, one of the young men who had recently been baptized, received word his mother had passed away. As he worked every day, there was no chance to return to his village to tell his family this great truth. The young man told my husband his mother had been filled with the Spirit but had not been baptized in Jesus' name before she died. He believed the Lord would raise his mother so she could be baptized in Jesus' name.

The young man told my husband he would work a day or two because he needed money for his family and then go home. Since he was the oldest son, the family would not bury her without his being there. Don and the young man made it a matter of prayer and we knew

God is a miracle worker. He left with confidence that God would raise his mother from the dead so she could be baptized.

After working two days, the young man took the night bus to his mother's area. Once off the bus, he walked quite a distance to his village. When he arrived, everyone was there for the funeral. In many parts of Africa, it was the custom of family and friends to gather at the home of the deceased and wait for the burial.

Thankfully, it was our cool season. The mother had been laid out in her little hut. The son went in and began to pray, telling the Lord his mother had never heard this truth of baptism; his village had never heard the truth.

God miraculously raised her from the dead. There was no small stir in that village. Even the chief came to see and he sent word for us to come and preach. Immediately we packed, picked up our children from school and got on our way.

After spending the night at a small old hotel in the area, next morning we traveled to the village. Many people were still at the home of the mother. The chief came as soon as he heard the missionary had arrived.

My husband had time to talk to him about this great message of truth. Later in the day, most of the village came for the teaching of the Word at the request of the chief. It was not a large village but there were many who heard the message of one God, baptism in Jesus' name, and the infilling of the Holy Ghost.

The young man's mother was walking and talking by the time we arrived at the village. She was soon baptized in Jesus' name. What a miracle she was to the land of Kenya.

Rejoicing, we returned to Nairobi. The next week my husband sent a couple of preachers to that village where they baptized over 100. Don always said, "It only takes one miracle to bring a revival." That was true in the book of Acts and it is still true today.

Water Attack

When we returned to Nairobi, school was on break. Don decided to take the children to the Mombassa seaside, one of their favorites.

The children were anxious to get into the water when we arrived. My husband went into the water and Keith did the same but went out further. All at once, he came up from the water fighting. Keith had been attacked by a large Portuguese Man of War. His Dad immediately went to help him. The tentacles had wrapped itself around Keith's arms and hands. At last, my husband was able to set him free. We immediately went to a private doctor because Keith is highly allergic to any kind of bites or stings. He was a very sick boy. Don and I took turns sleeping near him a few nights afraid his heart might stop. With prayers and care, he was all right in a few days.

Adventurous Bus Trip

God blessed us with the visit of Brother J. P. and June Hughes during the year the Harris family was on leave in the states. The Hughes were the furlough replacements for our Nigeria missionaries. When the missionary visas ended, they had to leave the country. While they were waiting for a new visa, Brother Freeman made arrangements for the Hughes family to stay with us in Kenya. Their visit proved to be blessing as they soon became lifelong friends and Uncle John Paul and Aunt June to our children.

Brother Hughes loved to play chess and so did my husband. Many evenings they had wonderful games. Sister Hughes was a great cook and an excellent friend. Brother and Sister Hughes loved to fish and, as often as possible, went with my husband and Keith to fish on Lake Naivasha. What a blessing Brother Hughes was with his anointed teaching and preaching.

Kelli hit it off with Sister Hughes immediately. One day she made a bus trip to town and took Kelli with her. When she pulled the bell to stop near the post office, the driver pulled over at the corner to let them off. Kelli was put off first but the driver did not wait for Sister Hughes to exit before closing the door and starting on his way. She was hollering, "Stop! Stop!" Kelli was running down the road chasing the departing bus.

Don's shoeshine boy saw Kelli running after the bus. He knew who she was since he always polished her Dad's shoes. Afraid Kelli would be hit by a car, he ran out to catch her. When he caught her, Kelli did not recognize him so she started hitting and kicking him. Quickly handing Kelli an orange Fanta soda and a chocolate bar, she slowly started calming down while they waited for the bus to stop.

Two blocks down the road, the bus driver pulled into the station and Sister Hughes got off the bus. Another shoe shine boy directed her to where Kelli was. She started running towards Kelli. By now, Kelli pulled away from the shoeshine boy and ran to meet Sister Hughes. A happy reunion took place in the middle of the road.

Dress for Grandmother

It was time for the Bible school to open. Brother and Sister Harris, my husband, and I would be teachers. However, we did not open the Bible school immediately because Brother Harris received word the school could not open until the headquarters' church was built. After contacting our Partners in Missions for financial help, we started the church by faith.

The church construction progressed daily. Workers made temporary one-room huts in our front yard. It was easier for them to stay there rather than making two daily trips to and from their homes. Some workers brought their families, young and old, to stay with them in the huts. It was a cold winter in Nairobi. Daily fires were made in our old home's fireplace. The workers used charcoal burners for cooking and heating. Workers set up near the construction where they hand chipped the large, beautiful local stones while singing. It was wonderful to awaken to these sounds.

Keith and Kelli were out of school for a few days. Kelli had made friends with the church workers' children and their families. Often she stopped to speak with an old grandmother. The grandmother wore a blanket all through the winter months. Never did I think anything about it since it was so cold. I knew she did not have a coat.

Awaking to a beautiful Spring morning, I got busy preparing food for our dinner guests that evening. About 10:00 a.m., Kelli came in to tell me the grandmother had washed her blanket and was sitting in the sunshine. I said, "That's nice," and went on chopping meat for our dinner. Kelli stood there for a few minutes and finally went back outside.

Around two o'clock that afternoon, Kelli came in again to let me know the grandmother had washed her blanket and was sitting in the sunshine. Two hours later the weather began to get cooler. Kelli came in once again to tell me the grandmother had washed her blanket; she was still sitting in the sun. I said, "That's nice."

"But Mama, she is naked!" wailed my daughter.

"Why didn't you tell me that?", I said

Kelli answered, "I told you over and over all day that she washed her blanket."'

I was sorry I had not been more aware of what Kelli was trying to tell me and told her I would give her a dress for the grandmother. Now I realized the grandmother had nothing under the blanket. Kelli was happy to take the dress to the grandmother. It was probably the best dress she ever owned, even though it was an old one.

Hilarious Culture Changes

After the completion of our headquarters church, we had a dedication for our new facilities. The Freemans and the Kilgores were special guests at our dedication. All the preachers from around the country came for this great event. Now, at last, we could officially open the Bible school.

Brother Harris and my husband had visited different areas of the country promoting the school during its construction.

Church leaders and board members attended classes and stayed in the dorms. Three students were from Ethiopia. One was from Zaire, now called the Congo. All were excellent students. Most of the students were from the western part of Kenya and had never lived in a city, nor had flush toilets, running water, showers or electricity. Some had never slept in a bed because they were used to a mat.

During our first school morning, we heard a loud scream. Looking outside, we saw one of the students, Steven, in the school yard in his birthday suit. My husband quickly went outside to see what was going on. Steven had turned on hot water for a shower and did not know how to turn on the cold water to get the right temperature, just about scalding himself. Leaving the shower running full blast, he ran outside, with water running down the stairs and out the front door. The trailblazer gave a lesson that morning on how to use the showers. Students had many new things to learn.

School had only been open a few days when someone came to tell my husband all the toilet seats were broken. He went to check. Sure enough, each of the toilets seats had a broken lid. He replaced them.

In a week or two, all the toilet seats were again broken. My husband could not figure out how the seats had been damaged. One of our students had been to the city and knew how the toilets worked. He told my husband the students had stood on the toilets, breaking them.

The students had a very special class that day on how to use the toilets. Inside our house I could hear loud laughing and hollering coming from a classroom. Rushing to see what was happening, I arrived just in time to see Don standing on a chair with both feet saying, "We do not stand on the toilet seat like this." My husband got down and sat on a chair saying "We sit on it like this or we stand in front of it." Everyone had a good laugh. There were no more broken toilet seats.

Devotion and prayer were held each evening. A regular mid-week Bible study was held with the students. Many times they took turns speaking and villagers were also welcome to attend.

Work duties were set up two hours a day for the students. Jobs were rotated - cooking, washing, busing dishes, cleaning tables, working outside, cleaning the toilets, and cleaning all the floors.

Students were surprised with their duties since most had never seen toilets and did not know how to clean them. Some had never boiled water, much less cooked.

Thursday nights were set aside to have dinner with all the students. Students prepared the meal and the Harris family often joined us. Usually I baked a cake for dessert.

One Thursday, Don asked me to make homemade ice cream since it was his favorite dessert. The students took turns cranking the manual machine. This was something they had never had. It was only available in the city.

Students served the ice cream while laughing and talking about how cold it was. All at once one of our students, Steven, fell on the floor groaning and rolling with pain in his head. My husband explained when you eat ice cream too fast, that is what happens. It is called brain freeze and is only temporary. At last, most of the students started eating their ice cream again, but much slower. One student passed his ice cream back to my husband and said, "Please heat it a little." Now he had the job of explaining that you could not heat the ice cream as it would melt.

Bible school days could be challenging. Don loved working with the students and his greatest desire was to see them grow in the ministry. My husband was a born mentor. Often he told me, "Jesus' ministry was pouring himself into his disciples." He thought he should follow that example.

Don was also a man of wit and wisdom. There were many daily problems in the school's beginning. Everyone was adjusting to new ways and customs.

One day a student came to him complaining that his roommate had stinking feet. Don went to check. Sure enough, he found a real bad odor in the room. He told the guilty party to wash his socks and feet every day. Still an odor prevailed.

Don returned to the room. This time, he instructed the student to wash his sheets and blankets. It helped but the student often forgot to wash his socks.

Down the hall another student had the same problem. This student was told to wash his socks, sheets, and blanket. Finally, my husband moved the two students who had stinking feet into the same room. It was not long until there were no more complaints. The guilty duo started washing their feet and socks daily.

Shocking Attire

There was always great excitement and a real blessing when a shipment of used clothes arrived from our mission partners. Shirts, pants, and shoes were distributed to the students. Some of the clothing was too big. A local tailor did a wonderful job cutting and remaking suits for the students. Brother Harris gave Steven a suit of his which the tailor took apart and made a nice suit.

Because the weather was colder in Nairobi than it was in other parts of the country, we tried to outfit each student with a jacket or sports coat.

Kenya received a lot of ladies' clothing which were distributed to our board members for their wives. Students were allowed to select clothing for their wives but they had no idea what size was needed. Sister Harris and I tried helping them choose something for each wife. It was a job yet everyone had a good laugh as they held up a dress to themselves to see if they thought it would work. Even a few single men tried to help them.

Unbeknown to us, one of the student's wives was expecting a baby soon. Her husband looked for something big enough and personally chose a dress, finding a long dress that had plenty of room

48

for her expanding midriff. The dress was long enough, there were some sleeves in it, and the neckline was not too low. Her husband thought it was a maternity dress and took his prized possession home.

The first ladies' conference in Kenya was to be held soon at our headquarters church. Women came from different areas of the country and traveled by bus. Since our Bible school was out for a long break, the ladies stayed in the dorms.

Keith was fifteen years old at this time. He came into the house to notify me one of the ladies had traveled from western Kenya and said, "She is pregnant and is wearing a long nightgown." He was very upset to think she came to a conference in a nightgown.

I told Keith, "No one knows it is a nightgown but you and I. Don't say anything and I will see the sister gets a dress for the services tomorrow."

Arriving at the service, I quickly realized why Keith had been so upset. The gown was pretty much see-through with nothing under it. The soon-to-be mother was extremely large with her pregnancy. A dress that would fit was found and given to her the next day.

Living at the Bible school and headquarters' ground, we never had a dull moment and were learning many things about the people and their customs.

Prayer for Rain

The Book of Acts was the class I taught and loved it. The doctrine class was my husband's specialty. As he was an excellent teacher, the class came alive.

It was easy for the African students to see one God and Jesus' name baptism. The trailblazer helped the Africans develop faith in their walk with God and in their ministry.

Many areas in the country were still experiencing severe drought. Women walked long distances to find drinking water. People and cattle were dying. There was no water to bathe and no water to baptize. The country was in dire straits.

Two men came from the Voi area to ask the church and Bible school to pray for rain. The students fasted and prayed. Our family joined in the prayer times.

A prayer chain was set up for the students to begin after school until the classes began the next day. In the beginning of the prayer chain, students tried to fill their time by singing and worshipping. Finally, they learned to fill in their time with all prayer.

These prayer meetings brought a good spiritual climate to our school. Their preaching became anointed and powerful. This helped bring a real spirit of unity. Prayer helped the students develop their ministry.

After a few weeks of the prayer chain, God marvelously brought the rain - plenty of water. Water for people, water for cattle, and water for baptism. The Lord opened up the heavens and poured out rain on that thirsty land. God sent the natural and spiritual rain. As the men began to be taught, we began to see real revival among our leaders and students.

Guests at the Gate

Late one evening there was a call from the gate. There stood three young men looking for the missionary who baptized in only one name, the name of Jesus. A lady had come to visit her family in Nairobi where they had witnessed to her. She had attended the church at the Y.M.C.A. and was filled with the Holy Ghost. The woman came to our monthly baptism service and was baptized in Jesus' Name. Upon returning to her village, she began witnessing to her pastor and others.

The lady's pastor began reading the book of Acts and he wondered about baptism on the day of Pentecost, searching the scriptures after the lady witnessed to him. He shared his finding with two of his minister friends. These three men traveled many hours by bus to Nairobi to find the missionary who would baptize them. While searching, they walked for two days trying to find the Bible school where we lived. Someone told them, "The missionary you are looking for is off Waiyaki Way near the Salvation Army compound."

Upon their arrival at the compound, they were told how to find us. It was late in the day when they arrived at our gate, hungry and very tired. My husband made a place for them at the school, fed them, and started teaching them that night. He continued an informal class the next morning after tea, giving them scriptures on one God baptism in Jesus' name.

The trio was baptized later that day. After returning to their village, they began teaching and preaching this truth. It was not long before we received word to come to their area to teach and baptize many of their people. The trailblazer once again took his family into a new area where revival broke out.

Bag of Tricks

The trailblazer loved the Bible school days. Many evenings following dinner, he and Keith would visit the students. Kelli would often join them for evening tea. Her Dad kept the students busy dividing them into teams, visiting and preaching in different areas each weekend.

One Saturday my husband took a team of students to a new village in the Machakos area where they were to have an open-air meeting, which my husband loved. This was a big day each week since every villager went to the market to buy or sell. Everywhere you saw ladies carrying vegetables and fruit on their heads to the open market.

A tree near the market was selected to have their service. The students began beating their drums and singing. People came by and stopped to enjoy the music.

Because not much went on in a village, many people were interested in our group. The students sang and then one of them preached a short time then they sang again, which made the crowd grow.

About this time, a witch doctor arrived setting up shop at a nearby tree. When he began beating his drum, many people who had stopped for our service, went over to see what the witch doctor was up to. Soon he took out his bag of tricks, as my husband called them. More people left our group and went to see the witch doctor.

The trailblazer told the students, "Keep beating your drums and singing. Keep worshipping." As they worshipped, the Spirit of God began to move and the villagers felt it.

Soon, the witch doctor ran out of gimmicks. The large crowd returned to our meeting. One of the students did the main preaching. At the end of the service, the preacher asked those who wanted prayer or needed God in their lives to step forward. Two or three received the Holy Ghost that day. One of these men later came to our Bible school.

Meet Mama

It was not long before we had a school break for the holidays. One weekend during the long break, my husband arranged for us to visit our church on a large sisal farm. There were rows and rows of little houses for the many workers and their families. The pastor of the church worked for the farm and also lived in one of the small houses.

Leaving early one morning, we drove three hours to arrive in time for the church service. It was blessed and there were several visitors because the missionaries had come. A lunch was prepared for us and some of the local church members. This type of visit was very useful, and one my husband and I enjoyed. It always gave my husband a chance to allow informal teaching to the pastors and leaders.

After waiting several hours, I decided to use the restroom before our long trip home since there were no toilets along the way. Privately, I asked the pastor's wife for directions. She walked into the room where all the men were sitting. In a big, loud voice she said, "Mama needs the toilet." The pastor spoke up and said he would take me. I responded, "No. I can find it if you just tell me where to go."

Because the pastor insisted, there was nothing I could do but let him take me since I was his guest. He felt responsible for me. He proceeded walking me between two long rows of little houses. People were sitting outside each house. At each eighteen or so houses, he stopped and greeted each person sitting outside while announcing, "I'm taking Mama to the toilet." By this time, I was totally embarrassed and turning red in the face.

When we finally reached the end of the row of houses, there was the long row of toilets (out houses) with half doors. Your head, shoulders, and legs were exposed for all to see. Because of my light coloring and height, I must have looked like a neon sign to them.

The pastor turned his back to me while stopping people coming to the toilets from all directions shouting, "Wait. Stop. I'm waiting on the Mama who is in the toilet." After that day, there was no more pride in me.

Returning to the house, it was time to say our goodbyes. The people begged us to come again and Don promised that we would come as soon as we could. On our way home, my husband continued to chuckle over my embarrassment.

Rat's Nest

Monday we were up and at it again, making sure there were supplies for the school kitchen. As school reopened that day, everyone was excited to tell what God had done in their villages during the school break.

Africa was good for our family. Evenings were enjoyable with our children. There were no electronic gadgets to keep everyone occupied. Always we had dinner together. If my husband was busy, we usually waited for him to return home before we ate. It was a rare thing for him to be late. Dinner time was when everyone shared what happened that day, at school, office, home or Bible school. Many nights the children played chess with their Dad.

Our large 55 year-old house with plenty of room for many guests, often had rats. The Freemans came through often on their way to other countries.

On one visit, Sister Freeman was resting on the couch. All at once, she saw a large rat. Brother Freeman told the kids to chase it down the hall and said, "I will jump on it with my cowboy boots."

A rat's nest had been found the previous day in our closet filled with several little ones. The mama rat had eaten the bottom of my best dress to line her nest. Don had cleaned out the nest but apparently missed the mama rat.

The kids chased the rat. When Brother Freeman realized it could run up his pants leg, he jumped in the air, and watched the rat run down the hall. Keith and his Dad took a mop and broom into the kitchen where they killed it.

In the near future, a family of mongoose moved into our yard and greatly diminished the rat population. The yard had several hens and one rooster as my husband had loved them since a child when he carted chicks (pullet size) around in his little red wagon. After the mongoose family took up residence, we did not have many eggs because they helped themselves. But, it was better than having rats and snakes in the yard.

Malaria Strikes

The trailblazer made his way to the eastern part of the country as often as he could. On one of these trips, we stopped in the Voi area for church services with one of our students, Brother Naphali. When we arrived, the saints were working on a much needed new grass roof for the church.

After leaving Voi, we traveled to the Mombassa area where my husband became sick with malaria fever. The following day Keith came down with it. Since our friends had moved, I asked around for a doctor knowing my husband and Keith needed medical attention. There was no doctor but there was an old nurse. By the time the nurse arrived with malaria tablets to reduce the symptoms, both were very sick. The next day the nurse told me, "The boy will probably make it, but not the man."

I stayed up four nights with them while earnestly praying, and God touched them. Don was still very weak. It took him a little while to recuperate from the malaria so we stayed a few days longer before traveling home.

Drastic Changes

When we returned home, a letter was waiting from Brother Freeman requesting us to visit a group of people in Zambia. There was a Church of God in Christ organization that had a good group of people. Brother Freeman had preached and baptized a few of them after headquarters had received a letter requesting more doctrine information. Someone from that organization had found one of our doctrine tracts on a path in Zambia with the church's headquarters Hazelwood, Missouri address. We never found where the track came from. Brother Freeman asked my husband to be the guest speaker at their 1977 conference.

Arriving late in the evening in Zambia, the bishop and another preacher met us at the airport with his car. Local preachers joined them in welcoming us to their country. My husband and I were driven to the Ecumenical Council Grounds in Kitwe where we were dropped off and were told they would return in two or three days. Since we had no phone, we had to trust them to come back for us.

On the fourth day of our stay, we were starting to get worried about their coming back. The preachers finally returned to take us to Mufulira. A large brush arbor-type building with branches lined the conference plot. We quickly realized why we did not see them sooner. The group had waited for the missionaries to arrive before making preparations. They were ready now to receive us and begin the conference.

By Sunday afternoon, the affect of my husband's teaching brought about a baptismal service. Water for baptism was quite a ways from the conference. People sang as they walked the road through the compound to get to the pond. Twenty-three people were baptized that day and thirty received the Holy Ghost during the conference. What a great victory.

Each day we walked or rode visiting different homes to pray for families. On the last day, they took us to an old African's home. Since he knew we were leaving and not sure when another missionary would be coming by, he called his children and grandchildren wanting us to pray for his family which meant praying for each member and to bless his home. This was their custom and it took quite awhile.

When our taxi came, the old man followed us. Before my husband got into the taxi, the old man threw himself down on his knees and wrapped his arms around him saying, "I am not going to let you go until you promise you will return and stay in Zambia to teach us more truth." Many of the preachers had gathered and began to beg us to return to Zambia.

The old man was not easily put off. He insisted on a positive answer. My husband said, "I cannot promise as we must have an appointment from our church in America."

He told the old man, "We will come if the Lord makes a way for us to come." At last, the old man let my husband go.

Upon returning to Kenya, we realized Zambia needed a missionary as they had no one to teach them truth. Leaving that country, we had a burden for the land and its people. That visit would bring a drastic change in our lives.

After my husband talked to Brother Freeman about his burden, he was allowed to apply for Zambia and to open that new mission field. He truly was a trailblazer, opening new churches, and reaching into new areas with this message because this was his passion.

The Donald Rivers family had received their appointment for Kenya at the last general conference. As we would be leaving for deputation in March, we received word that they were coming. We counted the days until their arrival.

The Rivers' shipment of goods came before their arrival. The shipping company sent a huge truck loaded with their things but rain and mud made it difficult to drive down our driveway. Bible school students unloaded all the appliances, couches, chairs, stove, washer, drier, and personal items on their heads. The rain made it difficult but they sang as they worked even though they were walking in mud up to their ankles. It would have been fun to have had a video of that sight. Thankfully, Sister Freeman was with us and directed their items to the correct place.

Time flew by. Soon it was time to say goodbye to our friends, the Harrises and Rivers.

When we finished our deputation, the Harris family was not ready for us in Kenya because they were waiting for the children's school semester to end. Since they needed more time, the trailblazer and his family took off for West Africa and Sierra Leone.

Unusual Pal

Arriving in Dakar, the capital city of Senegal, on Africa's West Coast, we visited our old friends, Brother and Sister Allard and their boys, staying two weeks. My husband preached a few services and God moved in a very special way. Keith stayed a few extra days to visit with the Allard boys.

Leaving Senegal, we flew to Freetown, the capital of Sierra Leone, where our friends, Brother and Sister Hughes, who were furlough replacements for the O'Keefe family met us. Previously, they had invited us to visit when we were waiting to travel to Kenya. Keith joined us in a few days. What a blessing it was visiting with them and my husband was happy to visit his chess-playing friend. Since the Hughes were staying in the O'Keefe's two-story house, there was plenty of room for us.

Nguli (pronounced "Ghouly"), the O'Keefe's chimpanzee, was a delightful blessing to our visit. Keith and Kelli had a great time being entertained by her. Soon we were to learn Nguli loved homemade peanut butter and we had to keep watch because she would help herself. Frequently, Keith and Kelli would take her for walks. The O'Keefes lived close to the sea, but Nguli hated water. If she saw the ocean, immediately she became afraid, hollering, making noises, and crying while quickly climbing onto the kids wanting to be held.

While we were there, Sister Hughes gave Kelli an adorable Spring hat with a wide brim which she enjoyed wearing to every service. The trailblazer preached in many of the little village churches. Our visit soon came to an end and it was time to leave for Kenya.

WAWA

After arranging to rent the Harris' furnished home while they were on deputation, we would arrive a few days before they left and would be looking forward to seeing our Kenyan friends, pastors, and saints.

Once we were onboard our plane to Kenya, we realized we were booked on the wrong flight due to a mix up. We had to stop in Ghana West Africa. The flight was going to Ethiopia and not Kenya. Since Ethiopia had much political trouble, it was unsafe for us to go there without visas.

Finding ourselves in Ghana without visas on a Sunday afternoon, we were told we had to wait until Monday since they were not issued on Sunday and the Money Exchange was closed. We were not allowed to leave the airport, nor allowed to make a phone call to the local missionary's home since we had no visas. After several hours, Don was finally permitted to use their phone.

While the missionaries, Brother and Sister Robert Rodenbush, were on deputation, Brother and Sister Chalet stayed in their home and cared for the Ghana churches. When my husband called their home, there was no answer. Later we learned they had gone up country for Sunday services.

Even though we were hungry, and most of all thirsty, we could not buy anything because we did not have their currency. The airport assigned an armed soldier to watch us. Late in the afternoon, Kelli and I needed to go to the restroom. Since the soldier spoke no English and I did not speak his language, I pointed in the direction of the ladies room. Finally, he understood what I was trying to tell him.

The soldier took us to the ladies' room and insisted he go inside with us. Once Kelli and I walked into the restroom, the soldier stuck his foot in the door. Quickly I pushed on the door and said, "No!" This continued a few times while trying to make him wait outside the door. The soldier persisted on following us into the restroom. I was just as insistent that he stay outside by the door. There was quite a tug of war going on at that door. I don't know where he thought we could run to since there was one tiny window inside, not large enough for a child to escape. Eventually, he relented and waited outside the restroom.

Don contacted Brother Chalet by phone late that evening, finally getting us released into his care until the following morning. Brother Chalet drove us to the home of the Rodenbush's where his wife had prepared a delicious meal, and we got a good night's rest. What an experience we had that day. It was a WAWA day. WAWA stands for the "West African Wins Again" slogan and is used to express frustration in a joking way when your plans change in ways you had no control over.

First thing the next morning, my husband and Brother Chalet went to the Immigration Office to get our visas. What wonderful fellowship we had as we visited with them for a few days until the next direct flight to Kenya.

The morning of our flight, we arrived early at the airport. Due to our flight being delayed, we waited several hours. What a relief when we were at last airborne.

No Bribe

Arriving very late in Kenya due to our delay, we were happy to have made it safely. How nice it was to be with our old friends, the

Harris family, the Rivers, and Sister Wendell. Soon we found ourselves teaching in the Bible school and traveling to the villages, having revivals along the way.

During the ten months that followed, we learned to love and appreciate the Rivers family. On one trip up country, the brothers went ahead to do some teaching and Sister Rivers and I were to follow them with the children at the end of the week.

Bible school students painstakingly tied the load of eight army cots and many pieces of luggage to the top of the station wagon. After traveling a few hours, we were stopped by a police checkpoint. Of course, they wanted to know what was on top of the car and we told them. A policeman said, "Take everything off so we can check it." This was his way to get a "gift" of shillings without asking for one.

I could not imagine how our two teenage boys would be able to reassemble everything. Sister Rivers looked at Keith and Jonathan, since they were the oldest, and said, "Boys, you will have to get it down."

The policeman finally realized he would not get a gift and said out of frustration, " Oh, you can go on!" With a big sigh of relief, we quickly climbed into the station wagon and continued on our way.

Once we got there, camp cots were set up in one of our interpreter's huts. The next week we had revival in villages where some of our students pastored. Three people received the Holy Ghost in the first service and nine in the next. On Sunday, the Lord came down in a powerful way and 35 received the Holy Ghost. Brother Rivers and my husband had preached in each village. God had blessed. We returned to Nairobi with victory.

Hen and Rooster

Upon returning to Nairobi, Bible classes were in session. Kenya had some very fine students who loved God and the truth.

The trailblazer felt led of the Lord to hold evangelistic meetings since there was a school break the next month. Sister Wendell was invited to join our family in the western area, with a stop in Molo where the power of God was poured out and 21 people received the Holy Ghost. Meetings were held in the Siaya area where 33 souls received the Holy Ghost. In the area of Nyanza, again we had an outpouring of God's Spirit.

A love offering was received from each church we visited. At one, our love offering was a live rooster for Keith, a live hen for Kelli, and a three foot stalk of bananas. The Kenyans always gave a rooster to males and a hen to females. My husband tied the chickens' feet together and put them in our trunk where they squawked all the way home.

The Bible school was ready to open when we returned to Nairobi. Everyone was very busy. It was time for the Harris family to return home. The Ikerd family would soon be on their way to Zambia. My husband flew to South Africa to pick up our station wagon, and drove to Zambia where the children and I met him.

Second in Line

Zambia was a new trail for the pioneer, Don Ikerd, the first resident United Pentecostal Church missionary. A year prior, the Freemans had arranged the purchase of our new vehicle. Since Zambia did not allow new cars into the country, they used our vehicle putting a number of kilometers on it before we arrived so it could enter as a used car.

Our departure for Zambia was almost a year late in our timing, but it was in God's perfect timing. If we had gone to Zambia before we had returned to Kenya, we would not have been able to get our automobile into the country. God alone knew when they were going to open the borders to South Africa.

Zambia's borders between the countries had been closed for seven years due to civil war. No vehicles had been allowed in. Don's Peugeot was the second vehicle in the first convoy allowed into Zambia. This was a historical day.

Vehicles were directed by a pilot car. The driver made sure cars were spaced out because the road had been filled with mines during the war. Soldiers had removed them but spaced the cars so they would not be too close to each other, just in case they missed one. It took several hours as their progress was very slow. Don prayed all the way that he would have no problems.

Our station wagon was loaded with food and supplies, as Zambia's supplies were short. A few kilometers from the border my husband noticed an old African man with white hair hitchhiking and pulled over to give him a ride. The old man got in the station wagon wanting a ride across the border but did not say much.

When they arrived at the border, there was much excitement. Newsmen and reporters were taking lots of pictures of the line of cars, especially the first one. When Don got out of his car to do the necessary paperwork, the old man also got out. Once the paperwork was completed, he returned to the station wagon where the old man was waiting.

Newsmen were still busy taking photos of the first car to cross the border. Don eased his station wagon up to the gate after declaring our goods. When the guard noticed the old African man in the vehicle, he lifted the bar and waved them on.

After driving a short distance, the old man said, "This is as far as I need to go." My husband looked around and noticed they were in the middle of no where, no huts, and no people around.

He asked the old man, "Are you sure?"

The old man said, "Yes. This is as far as I need to go."

Don pulled over and let him out. As he looked back, another car was coming so he quickly drove onto the road. When he looked again, there was no old man by the road. Surely the Lord had sent His angel to help get our station wagon and supplies across the border.

Adapting to Zambia

The children and I were waiting for my husband in Lusaka, the capital of Zambia. After picking us up at the airport, we drove to a small hotel. Next morning we went down for breakfast which consisted of only hot tea due to the shortage of food. There were no eggs, bacon, or bread available. After our quick breakfast of hot tea, we were on our way.

Driving from Lusaka to Ndola, we stayed in a small hotel next door to a butcher shop with an open door. Needless to say, it was difficult to miss the smell coming from the premises. Kelli, our sensitive-nose child, made us aware of the aroma.

Zambia had experienced a shortage of many food items for several years. Shopping for groceries would soon become a nightmare but we learned to stand in long lines for our daily needs. When bread was available, it was not wrapped. Each loaf had a three-inch piece of paper wrapped around it. This allowed you to pick it up but people did not do that. Everyone felt both ends of the bread to see if it was soft. After many fingers handled the loaves, the bread was definitely not germ-free.

The next day we met Bishop Mansaka in Ndola, formerly the national leader of the Church of God in Christ. He agreed to store our supplies at his house. Goods would disappear if we left them in our station wagon in full sight. Poor hotel security made it impossible to keep them there.

While building a relationship with the bishop, my husband started looking for a place that had two offices. A place was found with two rooms on a side street to use for offices. The bishop moved into one room. The trailblazer set up his office in the other where he could visit with all the preachers.

Our family stayed in the hotel two or three weeks until we found a large guest house that had one bedroom with three twin beds. At the guest house, Kelli shared our room. Keith slept in another. All the guests shared the kitchen and toilets. We did our own cooking. If you were late, you were the last to cook.

The first district meeting was held in mid-February at the Kansenshi Secondary School in Ndola. Over 300 people attended to meet the new missionary. Teaching oneness and Jesus' Name baptism were needed for the bishop's former organization of over 4,000 members. My husband did an outstanding job explaining the history of the United Pentecostal Church and what God was doing around the world. Many had not heard about Jesus' Name baptism. He spoke about the great message preached on the day of Pentecost.

God promised us if we came to Zambia and preached this message, many souls would be filled with a great outpouring of the Spirit of God. "Be glad then, ye children of Zion, and rejoice in the Lord your God: for he hath given you the former rain moderately, and he will cause to come down for you the rain, the former rain, and the latter rain in the first month. And the floors shall be full of wheat, and the fats shall overflow with wine and oil" (Joel 2:23-24). This promise we claimed as our work began in that country.

The land of Zambia was thirsty and the people were spiritually thirsty. "My soul thirsteth for thee, my flesh longeth for thee in a dry and thirsty land, where no water is" (Psalms 63:1).

Many things were learned at that district meeting about the old organization and how it operated in the past. Also, we were able to meet many people and more of our preachers.

We lived at the guest house but were desperate to find a place of our own. Because it was too expensive to ship our furniture to Zambia, it was left in Kenya. Brother Rivers made us a small wooden crate in which he loaded our personal items and air freighted them to Zambia.

Soon we realized every available rental house had already been booked by large companies for staff housing. The companies were willing to pay any amount of money, so this made for unbelievably high rent. After six weeks searching for a house, we found a man who was in charge of housing for the phone company. The company had three houses that had been booked, deposits paid, and were being held for incoming staff. After talking with this man several times, God moved on him to let us rent one of the houses and said, "I don't know why I am letting you have one." Yet, we knew our God was working on our behalf. What an answer to prayer.

Home at Last

After finally finding a house, we were very excited. The old house was located in a good neighborhood. It had three bedrooms and a large living room big enough for Don's Bible classes. With only our suitcases and supplies from Kenya, we moved into the house. An old lovely guava tree was in the front yard with a wash room in the back yard.

Since our house had many windows, people from the guest houses loaned us curtains, all different colors and styles. Their friends with the Evangelical church loaned us a wringer washing machine.

It was time to start the process to have Likes Line Shipping Company transport our shipment from New Orleans which would cost $17,000 American dollars and they could not guarantee safe delivery due to many hijackings at that time. The transportation company could only bring our items to Lusaka.

The Foreign Missions Department allowed each missionary a specific shipping budget. There were not enough funds to have our items shipped to us. By now, the shipping company had begun charging us storage because our shipment had been at the dock too long.

Fern, my sister, and her husband, Dennis, offered to pick up the shipment in New Orleans, and try to sell some of our items. Everything we needed was in that shipment, even a brand new bedroom set that a brother in Texas had given us.

One morning Don went to the post office to call Brother Judd, to let him know there was no way we could have our things shipped to

Zambia due to the cost. Brother Judd wanted to talk to me to make sure I was okay with that. Since we did not have the money, I agreed.

Money to buy new furniture was not in the budget, but Brother Judd was not told that. With the money we had, we started looking for used furniture. Expatriates leaving the country were a good source and we found a couch and a chair. My husband went to see the lady at the hotel where we had stayed, to see if there were any extra beds she would sell. The woman graciously loaned us two single beds and two extra mattresses, which we put on the floor for our children. Keith slept on that mattress until he went to the states for school later that year. Often I thanked God for our years of home missions as it helped us adjust.

A small fridge rental was found which would keep one small ice tray or a small chicken. Moving in with a make-shift table and chairs, we set up housekeeping.

The trailblazer started special teaching at our house on Saturdays for all the Zambian copperbelt ministers. These lessons proved to be a real blessing to the new baby church.

Opposition Begins

After being in the country a little over six weeks, one Sunday morning we came out of service to find several very angry men who opposed our coming to Zambia. Their leader was a Kenyan former boxer who started verbally picking on my husband saying, "Who invited you here? Who do you think you are?" The leader tried to aggravate my husband with words because he wanted to start a fight.

The trailblazer did not get upset and would not fight. Grabbing my husband's tie, the leader started choking him. Some of the saints and a few ministers pushed him away. Others joined in and broke up the men who were there with their leader, telling them to leave him alone. The group of angry men finally left.

The very next Sunday the same men followed us to one of the little village churches. They caused such a commotion that the police from the station down the road came to see what was going on. Police took all of us down to the station and finally told the men to leave the church and missionaries alone. These men were desperate to get us put out of the country, as they knew their illegal bakery scheme would come to light.

Who's There?

Soon after we moved into our Ndola home, I went to the wash room one morning with a load of dirty clothes. A noise was coming from the wash room but there was no one else at home. Calling out I asked, "Who's there?"

There was no answer. Calling out again, there was still no answer. Putting down my basket, I opened the door a crack and saw the largest cobra snake I had ever seen. It was as long as the wash room. Thank God I remembered to shut the door so it could not get out and hollered, "Snake! Snake!"

The little yard boy from next door heard me and called over the fence asking, "What's wrong?"

I told him there was a very long snake in my wash room. Quickly he scaled the fence and looked at the snake through the open wash room window. Returning to the yard, he picked up rocks. Bringing them back, he threw rocks through the open window, hitting the snake in the head until it lay still. After awhile, he opened the door and went inside where he cut off its head with his panga, a machete knife, that was used for yard work. Snake problems continued but we prayed God's protection on our children.

Setting the Pace

The trailblazer continued teaching doctrine at our house on Saturdays. The classes helped open the eyes of the men who truly loved God and had a desire to walk in truth. Little by little, they began to open up and ask questions, which led to discussion of more scriptures. Some of the men began to see they needed to be baptized in Jesus' Name. When we first met them, some brought their baptismal certificates to us which stated they had been baptized in Jesus' name. Later, we learned the leaders and preachers were given the certificates stating they had been baptized in Jesus' name before we came, but had never been baptized.

One Sunday afternoon we had a baptism for a few of the local saints. My husband invited all the brothers to attend. The presence of the Lord came down as we began to worship and some were filled with the Holy Ghost in the water.

The trailblazer finished baptizing and was standing in the water. Everyone was still worshipping the Lord. When I looked up, Brother Sonkani was walking in the water towards my husband saying, "I need to be baptized in Jesus' Name." After borrowing someone's wet clothes in which they had been baptized, he was the first to step forward from the old group. Brother Sichivula and Brother Mendia were baptized in Jesus' name by the next baptismal service. Several others came forward to be baptized. The Lord was revealing this truth to hungry hearts.

Following that baptism, Brother Sichivula invited us to his home for a Bible study. His wife was a stanch Catholic and had never been to church with him. When we went to their little house, my husband taught on receiving the gift of the Holy Ghost. After teaching, we had prayer. As we were praying with his wife, she received the Holy Ghost. What a blessing she was to his ministry and became a great pastor's wife.

One day when Keith and his Dad went to pick up mail, a notice arrived that our appliances, purchased by the Mothers' Memorial Fund, were on their way at last from South Africa. The morning the appliances arrived, there was great excitement in our home. Keith skipped through the house shouting, "Yippee, yippee! Iced tea, iced tea!" Americans love our iced tea and my husband loved iced tea more than any of us, always teasing the kids about savoring a glass of iced tea or Coke with chilled sweat running down the outside.

Don found a house that was in line with our budget and we quickly moved into it. It was not long before we realized God had directed our step and had placed us where we needed to be.

Vaccinations Required

When Keith drove his Dad and the bishop in the country of Zaire, the police always stopped him to see if he had a driver's license. He had a Zambian one and an international driver's license. Each time they traveled to Zaire, immigration officers asked to see their immunization records to prove they had current shots.

The bishop and my husband arranged to attend a special meeting where many denominations had been invited to hear this one-God message. What a move of God they had. Afterwards, some of the Trinitarian preachers desired to be baptized. When it was time to leave, everyone begged them to return soon.

Arriving back at the Zambian border, the immigration officer stopped Keith, my husband, and the bishop. He told them their cholera shot had not been taken on time and would not allow them to enter Zambia for another three days. The trailblazer talked and talked but the man would not budge. At last, he asked the officer, "Where do you live?"

The officer said, "I live in a little house at the border post."

Don told him, "We will come and stay at your house for three days, as we have no where to stay."

The officer stomped his feet and yelled, "You can't do that!" Quickly he stamped their passports and let them return to Zambia.

Puddy

Green and black mamba snakes were a problem at our new house. One day Keith came home with a very tiny kitten after finding it on a walking path. I never liked cats and did not want it. The kids begged their Dad to keep it. He finally said they could and told me, "It's okay as it is too small to make it without its mother."

The children took turns getting up at night every hour to feed her with a nose dropper. Even though the kitten made it, for a time she lost all her hair, looking like a mouse and then a rat before she grew bigger. Finally, the kitten grew into a nice-looking outdoor cat.

At the time, I did not realize God had answered our prayers about the snakes in our yard. As the kitten grew, she began to kill snakes. Once in a while she would drag them to the porch so we could see she had done her duty.

After quite a while, we started calling her Puddy. She was white with gray spots. Often we had rats come in from the nearby field but there were less since Puddy came to stay. I told my husband, "I would rather have the cat than snakes or rats."

One day I saw a large rat in our bedroom. When my husband came in for lunch, he put Puddy in the bedroom for awhile, hoping she would find the rat. After returning to the bedroom, Don saw no rat. The window was open so he assumed Puddy had chased the rat out the window.

An errand took him to the post office. Upon returning home, he went into the bedroom to lie on the bed and read The Pentecostal Herald that had come in the mail. When he raised up with his elbow on the pillow and felt something moving, he thought it must be the cat still looking for the rat. After reading for awhile, he left the bedroom.

That night after bathing and ready for bed, I moved the pillow and there was the dead rat. Apparently my husband had smothered the rat with his elbow. I let out a loud scream and everyone came running.

Untimely Death

One morning at his office, the trailblazer found papers in the outside trash. Apparently whoever threw them in the trash never thought anyone would find them. The papers exposed a bakery scheme

(African word for project) in the name of the United Pentecostal Church International.

Don told me he knew some of the men on the church board were involved in illegal businesses in the country and felt Bishop Mansaka knew of these things. Men involved were very angry about our coming into their country and wanted the bishop to help them remove us from Zambia because they were afraid their actions would be discovered.

The new missionary to Zambia spent a lot of time traveling to new areas with the bishop, teaching several Bible studies at his home, and ministering to him daily. Bishop Mansaka was well known, loved, and respected in the city.

One morning I heard a knock at our gate. The yard boy went to the gate to see who was there. It was Vance, the bishop's oldest son. When he learned Keith and his Dad were gone to town, he asked to talk to me. Vance came in and began to tell me his father was very sick and in the hospital. The bishop had sent word by his son for us to come immediately.

The Ikerd family had only been in the country six months. There was no way to call my husband since there were no cell phones. Instructing Vance to go to the office to see if my husband was there, I reassured him we would pray and come as soon as he returned. As I prayed, I thought of the bishop and all the interpreting he had done for my husband. The two of them had traveled every day or worked in the office together and had become close friends. When Bishop Mansaka had visited our home the previous night, he did not seem to be sick. Leaving our house, he told us he planned to see friends before going home.

Thank the Lord it was not long until Keith and his Dad arrived home. We went at once to the hospital. Since it was not visiting hours, the hospital let us in because we were missionaries. Once we saw the bishop, we could tell he was very sick. After praying for him, the bishop had two requests: go to Chingola and bring Brother Sonkani to the hospital, and he did not want to be left alone. My husband asked me to stay while he was gone. A message was sent to the bishop's wife, Mama Mansaka, who was at the Children's Hospital with little Dorcas, their baby, who had been severely burned requiring a three-week stay.

The trailblazer left immediately to find Brother Sonkani but he had never been to his house by himself because the bishop had always traveled with him. It was a two-hour trip but my husband managed to find his house.

Since I had not heard from the bishop's wife, I asked the nurse to put through a call to the Children's Hospital. Two board members who worked in town were called. When one of the brothers arrived, he left immediately to get Mama Mansaka who was waiting on a family member to come to stay with their daughter, Dorcas.

When Bishop Mansaka was taken for some tests in the next room, he told me, "Don't leave me." I assured him I would stay. Hearing voices in the next room, the bishop sat up to look out the curtain, wanting to make sure I was there. By the time the nurse returned the bishop to his room, he seemed to be worse and unable to speak.

Mama Mansaka arrived and tried to talk to him but he did not say much. Sitting on the end of his bed awhile, she then sat on the floor. The bishop passed away before my husband and Brother Sonkani arrived. Often we wondered if he would have told Brother Sonkani what had happened to him since he had trusted him.

I waited with Mama Mansaka until my husband and Brother Sonkani arrived. The bishop was only 37 years old. His death was mysterious and untimely. My husband and I felt he had possibly been caught up in something out of his control. The bishop had realized with all the teaching the trailblazer had done, he did not want any part of what was going on. The men involved would let nothing and no one stand in their way.

African Funeral

African funeral customs are quite different but witchcraft is eliminated from Christian funerals. We had attended African funerals but had never been a part of one.

As was the custom, the bishop's funeral lasted four days and nights. African funerals are affairs in which the whole community feels the grief of the bereaved and shares in it. Beds and living room furniture were removed from the deceased's house to make room for seating. All the women sat on the floor. Men and boys stayed outside. A bonfire was built in the yard, as it was the end of July and still cold in Zambia.

During the time preceding the funeral, visits were paid by people in the community coming to pay their respects and offered condolences to the family. In the case of Christians, a nightly vigil was a time of comfort and encouragement. Radio announcements were made daily notifying friends and family of the bishop's funeral since no one had a phone.

Each night we left and returned the next morning bringing bread, tea, milk, and sugar. The church fed a very large crowd each day, approximately 250. At last, the day of the funeral arrived. It was one of the largest funerals I had every seen. It was customary for the family or church members to wash, dress the body, and place it in a wooden coffin.

One of the family members started to take the bishop's watch and my husband said, "No. That is for his son." Some tried to take his clothes but again he told them it was for his son. Keith was seventeen at this time and loved the bishop. He begged his Dad to allow him to put on the bishop's tie after they had dressed him. This was the first dead person Keith had ever touched. Afterwards, he broke down and cried.

The main funeral service was to be held at a rented church building. Since the crowd was too large, the funeral service was moved to the gravesite. A procession of 400-500 people marched to the funeral. This was something to see. The car had to be parked at the front of the cemetery. We walked a long way to the site.

Arriving at the gravesite, the family and brethren had dug the grave. The casket was lowered into the ground followed by a short graveside service. When the burial prayer was finished, people began filling in the grave with dirt. Many people took turns picking up dirt, throwing it in, and some shoveling it in.

Kelli and I started for the car when they were finishing the burial so we did not see what happened next. My husband told us after the funeral what had transpired. While they were filling the grave, a young man picked up dirt and put it in his pocket. The crowd thought it was for witchcraft purposes and believed that whoever he would put the dirt on would be the next to die. The entire crowd was extremely angry and wanted to beat him. The young man started to run away. Kelli and I could hear the crowd running and screaming.

Suddenly, I looked up and saw a young man in his early twenties making a beeline for me. He made a running tackle like they do in a rugby game, almost knocking me over. The crowd had sticks and stones to beat him but they could not get to him because of me. He kept screaming, "Mama, save me! Mama, save me!"

Even though the young man was unknown to me, I could not let them beat him to death. About that time, my husband arrived. When he saw what was taking place, he told the crowd they could not take the law into their own hands, reassuring them he would personally take the young man to the police station and let them deal with the problem. It took a lot of talking. By now, some of the preachers and saints realized they could not beat the young man to death. Eventually, we were able to get him into the car but he would not let me go. The young man knew his life was worth nothing without protection. Still scared and clinging to me, I got in the back seat with him.

At the police station, he was arrested and put in jail, probably to protect him as much as anything. The court often tried witchcraft cases in Zambia.

Help Wanted

Without the bishop to help us interpret, we were now on our own. Right after the funeral, the group of men who were against us took their complaints to the government with a list of accusations against my husband. A notice summoning him to court came in the mail. Accusations were that he was a racist and that he had brought false doctrine into the country - all lies.

Help was needed and we did not know where to turn or whom to trust. Prayer and fasting were the first things we did. When legal aid was sought, the lawyer told him, "Pastor, if you do not have people to stand with you, I advise you to leave the country."

We were desperate for help. One day Don said to me, "Let's go and see if Brother Sonkani will come and help us." He knew the bishop had trusted him. Eventually we learned he was not part of the illegal business.

At once we left so we could return by dark. As we drove, we continued praying for the Lord to lead us and give us someone to travel around the country to obtain signatures of people who wanted us in the country. Finally, we found Brother Sonkani's home. The front door was closed and it looked like no one was home. Don asked me to go to the door which I did, but there was no response. Knocking again, there was still no answer, but I heard people talking in the backyard. I asked my husband to turn off the motor and come with me. Reaching the backyard, Brother Sonkani saw me and said, "Mama."

I said, "We need your help."

Brother Sonkani was willing to go with us even though he had not been around us very much since he lived too far away. He had been faithful to our Saturday teachings. His English was good and could translate and interpret for the trailblazer. When we left that day, he went with us not realizing it would be a few weeks before he was able to return home.

The duo set off the next day to obtain the signatures needed to present to the court. Proof was needed the missionary was wanted in the country. The trailblazer was shining a beacon on new trails across Zambia while visiting little villages where he had preached and other areas he had not visited. That trail led them from the north, south, east, and west.

At last, they had enough names, addresses, and signatures to defend my husband and let the government know he was wanted in the country. They returned in time for the court hearing.

All the required paperwork was given to the judge. After that meeting, the opposition group contacted the World Council of Churches to help them put the new missionary out of the country. The men were relentless in their pursuit. It took awhile for them to come up with anything else. The World Council of Churches stepped into the fight because they felt they had the power to stop us.

Men Plotting

By now, our church board had dismissed three men from the board due to their immorality. This trio reported my husband again to the authorities accusing him of wrongfully dismissing them. The men had been the board's assistant superintendent, secretary, and treasurer with signature power. These men were very upset with their dismissal. The new missionary was filling in as the superintendent at this time and had not been officially installed.

While the trio and their leader, an outsider, were still plotting against us, we were in need of a superintendent. We were waiting on Brother Freeman to come for the voting. Thankfully, things quieted down a little. Beforehand, threats had come in writing, and some by word of mouth to our preachers and saints. Threats were even made towards our children, which we never let them know. These men were willing to do anything to get us out of the country because we were a threat to their illegal dealings. We were trusting in the living God. Don was a man of great faith. Faith kept us through all these storms.

No Man in the House

It was time for Keith to go to the states for his senior year. He would travel with his Dad and Brother Sonkani to the World Conference, then on to the states. Keith was going to South Dakota to stay with my sister, Fern, and her husband, Dennis Uecker. It was hard to let him go since he had never been away from home. Keith had been a great blessing to us.

It had been arranged for Mama Sonkani to come and stay with Kelli and I so we would not be alone while my husband was out of the country. Kelli was delighted that Mama Sonkani came with her brand new baby girl, Gladys. Kelli called her Gigi and it stuck. She was such a tiny little one. While the brothers were out of the country, I walked Kelli to school and back since we were having troubles in the country. No one could be on the streets after dark.

Late on Saturday afternoon, a car arrived in our driveway. Three men came to ask me to go with them to pray for a brother who was very sick in Luanshya. The men told me to come and bring Kelli along.

As I walked to the gate, the Lord warned me. I told them, "We cannot go, as it is late and could not get back in time." Two of the men I knew, the other one I did not. He got out of the car to persuade me to go with them. About that time, Mama Sonkani came out of the house. They had no idea she was there. She told them I could not go and at last they left. Word got out a few days later these men had not intended to bring us back home. Through everything that happened, God kept His hand on us. My husband and Brother Sonkani returned from the World Conference a few days later. We were very thankful to see them.

Peace Officer

At this time, the opposition group was still plotting against us. Zambia was much in need of an official superintendent. Brother Freeman came to the voting where he suggested they put in Brother Ikerd, but the board wanted to put in one of their own men. Brother Freeman said "Okay, but whoever you put in, I will take his name back to headquarters. We will need to investigate the man you put in to represent the United Pentecostal Church International."

After they talked among themselves, they agreed to vote on Brother Ikerd as his background had already been checked by the international church board and the Foreign Missions Board. He was voted in as superintendent.

After Brother Freeman left, we were on our own again. Our situation became a matter of earnest prayer. The last part of James 5:16 says, "... the effectual fervent prayer of a righteous man availeth much." The trailblazer felt God would help us clean up the board since there were still some men on the board who were not qualified. His new position helped him keep peace among the board members. Prayer would bring it about in a way that we would see victory and revival in the church of Zambia.

Signatures Don't Lie

One Monday morning, Don went to the bank. While there, a staff member came over to ask him about paying the monthly church loan that was overdue. My husband told her that he was not aware of any loan. The clerk explained the bank had loaned the church quite a sum of money for a bakery scheme (project). The loan was supposed to create jobs for people in the area.

Asking to see the signatures on the loan, she showed him. Sure enough, a trio of church board members had taken out a loan without my husband's knowledge. The loan papers showed the signatures of the church board's assistant superintendent, secretary, and treasurer. Also, the leader of the opposition group's signature, a non-board member, was there.

Don told the bank staff member he was the superintendent and his name was not on the loan. He told her the board had never had a meeting to vote on such a loan since he had been installed. She agreed to make a copy of the document which had the loan details and gave it to my husband. These signatures would, several months later, clear the church of the loan.

Trial Days

The World Council of Churches went to the government again and brought false charges against the trailblazer trying to do everything they could to make him leave the country. A court date was set where he would have to appear before the district judge.

This council called other denominational churches inviting them to this hearing but did not tell my husband. Arriving at court, several men were there from other churches. When the judge began asking my husband questions about the board's dismissing the men, he asked the judge why the other church leaders were there. The judge said they had not been invited by him or his office, but by the World Council of Churches. My husband told the judge it was not a matter to be discussed with outside churches; it was an internal matter. Since the judge did not have time to review the paperwork, another date was set because of charges from the Council of Churches stating three former board members had not been tried fairly or in love. The judge requested the men be retried before the next court meeting.

Another church board meeting was scheduled according to the judge's request even though the men had already been tried two times. Now the church had paperwork showing the illegal loan as proof of misconduct and wrongful signing that had never been board-approved. The board again found them guilty of misconduct, as well as wrongfully signing a loan in the name of the United Pentecostal Church International.

It was a very painful and hard time for the new Zambian baby church. Those three men visited our little churches and made false accusations against Brother Ikerd thinking the churches would side with them. It hurt our church. A few people left, and some did not trust the new missionaries.

The judge only gave us a few days to have the new trial. Once the trial started, the opposition group accused the deceased Bishop Mansaka of signing and arranging the loan. Our lawyer brought the original signed loan papers to this hearing. The World Council refused to accept our board's third decision to dismiss the men, saying they had not been judged in love and demanded the men be retried with one of their council members present.

Again, the judge asked my husband, "Will you retry the men one more time and have a representative from the World Council of Churches there?" He agreed.

Don remembered meeting a young man in Ndola who was the council's representative on the copperbelt and lived between Ndola and Mufulira. Asking around for directions to the man's house, he drove out to find him, requesting the man to come to the next church board meeting. The man agreed to come and represent the World Council of Churches.

No place was available to hold the board meeting so we held it in our living room. Once again, the board found the trio guilty of immoral conduct as well as wrongfully taking out a loan in the name of the church. The men they retried were very angry and gave the board a hard time.

At the hearing a week or two later, the World Council of Churches refused to except their representative from the copperbelt and insisted Brother Ikerd have a member of their executive board present. The council informed the judge my husband had brought false doctrine into the country. The judge asked, "What doctrine?"

The World Council of Churches Secretary replied, "The new way of baptism in only one name, the name of Jesus." Don inquired if he had ever read the book of Acts. When he said he had, my husband asked, "How did Peter baptize on the day of Pentecost?"

The secretary responded, "Peter was drunk on the Spirit and made a mistake."

The trailblazer replied, "Then Paul had to be drunk with the same Spirit because he baptized the same way, in the name of Jesus."

Because there was such dissention in the court room, the judge demanded the trial be taken to Lusaka, the capital, where the World Council of Church's main office was located. The court set a date for early the next month as the judge was fed up with all the complaints and accusations.

The Battle is the Lord's

The missionary had the job of investigating the illegal church loan and reviewing the bakery scheme (project), which was supposedly the reason for the loan. Property had never been purchased. It had been an illegal scam presented to the bank in order to get a large loan. The group of men who submitted the loan assumed they would not be turned down if it was processed in the name of the international church. They assumed the international church would have to repay it. The bank was unaware of this. The opposition group wanted to remove my husband from the country so he could not stop their scams.

The trailblazer was a man of faith and knew God had sent us to Zambia. He had no doubt the Lord would take care of us. There were some mighty promises in the Word of God that he stood on. One promise was found in Deuteronomy 20:4: "For the Lord your God is he that goeth with you, to fight for you against your enemies to save you." My husband said, "No matter what charges, the Lord will fight for me." His calm spirit is what helped him through all the trials and accusations never getting upset or shouting in anger.

The judge had requested the loan papers be presented to court with the illegal signatures ahead of time and a copy of our international church's Constitution and By Laws. Court requested our church board member qualifications so they could be carefully examined. The opposition group was to submit their complaints and accusations.

We went home to fast and pray and let God fight our battle. Another great promise God gave us was found in Isaiah 43:1-7. Verse two says, "When thou passest through the waters, I will be with thee and through the rivers they shall not overflow thee: when though walkest through the fire thou shalt not be burned; neither shall the flame kindle upon thee." What a promise. There were many times we felt like we were walking through a fiery trial yet were never burned.

At last, the court date arrived with many people in attendance. The World Council of Churches was well represented, with most of their executive board members present. One of their greatest complaints was we did not belong to their organization. They called my husband a racist and said he had brought false doctrine to Zambia. But, when our paperwork was brought out with signatures on the illegal loan, there was not much they could say. The late bishop could not be blamed since his signature was not on the loan. The judge ordered in favor of our Zambian church and told the World Council he did not want to see them again. It was finished. God was on our side. This was a victorious time for our church.

Opposition Moves to Lusaka

Court trials came to an end, but our opposition still continued to fight us.

The three men and their leader were very angry. The disposed men did not take it well because they had lost their positions among the church people, power, honor, and monetary benefits. Don had accidentally found proof of a large loan they had signed in the name of our international church. The men had counted on that money for their illegal bakery scam. Cash from the loan financed forged traveler's checks in neighboring countries, reaching Ziare, Tanzania, and Kenya.

Nothing would stop the opposition. They now turned to witchcraft out of revenge against my husband and the church. Yet, it was a big relief to know that Don would not be summoned back to court since he was able to find proof of the men's names on the illegal loan.

The board voted in new leadership who had stood with us through all these months. Men who were filled with the Holy Ghost who loved and lived the truth. Now was the time to train our ministers.

When Brother Freeman had installed my husband as the new superintendent a few months prior, he told him it would be best to move to Lusaka, the capitol city. A Bible school was needed for ministerial training. We listened to his words of wisdom and felt the opposition group would lay low awhile. There was a possibility these men would be tried for their illegal loan since the bank was pressing charges. Now was the right time to move to Lusaka.

Immediately, the trailblazer looked for land to build a Bible school and church. Don had heard the city offered ten-acre plots that had been approved for churches. When he went to the city offices to check on them, he was told there were none available, even though he had learned other churches had been given plots. Later, my husband learned the opposition group had gone to the city and made complaints about him and the international church. One of the men from that group had a friend on the city council and persuaded him to vote to deny our request. The opposition was still working against us, but we claimed victory in the name of Jesus.

Delayed One

Keith was gone to the states to finish his last year of high school. Kelli had made friends with Mavis and Peggy, two girls down the street. Frequently she talked to Peggy's older sister, Mrs. Lumina, who was raising Peggy like her own child because their mother had died shortly after her birth.

During a conversation with Kelli, Mrs. Lumina, said her husband was going to take a younger wife because she could not have children. They had been married for twelve years without a child. Kelli told her, "You need to go and see my mother."

The next afternoon she was at my gate and I invited her in. Mrs. Lumina was a registered nurse, schooled in England. Her husband was in charge of the largest government grocery store in the country, ZCBC, and lived only a few houses from us and were people of means.

As we talked, I said, " I serve a God who is able to do all things because nothing is impossible with Him." I shared with her the Bible story about the little lady who sought help from doctors for twelve years, yet she was still in need of healing. One day Jesus came to her village. When she saw him, she made up her mind to reach out and touch him for healing. (Mark 5:5-29)

Mrs. Lumina was so desperate to have a child that she had gone to a very prominent Malawi witch doctor who had put her in a large pot of herb-laced water and lit a fire under it. When it got too hot, she jumped out of the pot. Afterwards, she still did not get pregnant. Another witch doctor mixed a concoction of strong thick and green herbs to drink but it made her very sick. Still no baby.

After telling me this, she broke down and cried and I prayed with her. Since she did not know about receiving the Holy Ghost, I shared with her. Mrs. Lumina became hungry for the Spirit of God in her life. After inviting her to come to an all-night prayer meeting at the end of the week, she left promising to go with us.

On Friday she was at our gate ready to go. We arrived at the little house in the compound for the prayer meeting which was held in a temporary room set up in the yard made from tin sheets. People stood worshipping God and praying. The prayer meeting was greatly blessed and God began pouring out His Spirit. About 2:00 a.m. I was praying with Mrs. Lumina and my husband joined me. He laid hands on her and prayed and others gathered around. All of a sudden, she began to speak in tongues. Oh, what joy filled her life. Returning home the next morning, she was a new person. Sister Lumina quit drinking, started coming to church, and became a very faithful Christian.

Several months later she attended our General Conference which was held in Lusaka. Sister Lumina asked my husband if they could have special prayer at the conference for her to have a child. He told her there would be a special prayer line on Sunday afternoon for that purpose.

Brother and Sister Freeman arrived for the General Conference. God moved mightily in our conference and people were filled with the Spirit. Some were baptized on that Sunday afternoon. The special healing line was arranged.

The trailblazer had talked to Brother Freeman about Sister Lumina's prayer request prior to the service. At the end of the regular healing line, Brother Freeman asked if anyone wanted prayer to have a child. Sister Lumina came forward and another lady, Sister Longwe. We were trusting the Lord for miracles.

Right after the conference Sister Lumina's husband was transferred to Kasama where he managed the ZCBC store. Since there was no church in Kasama, my husband encouraged her to start a Sunday School and prayer meeting in her home.

Mr. Lumina insisted his wife return to his denominational church. She agreed but when she informed him she would return to her old way of life - drinking and partying - he said he did not want that to happen since there had been a real change in her life. Mr. Lumina told her, "You can start having services in our home."

Both ladies had had special prayer to have a child at the General Conference about ten months earlier. Sister Lumina gave birth to a big baby boy. Sister Longwe gave birth to a baby girl one week later. These babies were miracles. Sister Lumina named her son Chamuka, which means the delayed one. Faith in God includes faith in his timing.

Orchard Fire

The Ikerd family moved to the Evangelical Compound in Lusaka Zambia. One Sunday afternoon, my husband and I lay down for a nap. While we were sleeping, Kelli took the trash out to dump in our large, deep pit. The office had told us to always be sure to burn the trash each time because it was a place for snakes to live. That day we had a strong breeze. Kelli built her fire as usual but it quickly flared out of control heading for the nearby mango orchard.

Awaking to hear Kelli yell at Ruthy, her friend, to quickly get a bucket of water, I thought I had better get up to check on them. Once outside, I quickly called to my husband, "Come quick!"

Don ran out the door, saw what was happening and yelled, "Fire. Come and help!" Men on the compound rushed to put out the blaze. The volunteer fire department could not help us since we were too far from town. Most of the field burned but the Lord, our Protector, did not let it spread to the houses on the compound.

First Registration

The trailblazer traveled many times to the Lusaka city offices to seek a plot of land for the Bible school and church since he had heard 10-acre plots were being issued to churches. Each time he visited the response was always, "There are none available." Never did he get tired, discouraged or upset.

While waiting and praying for one of the plots, he visited the city offices to check the procedure to get our church registered in Zambia. The city office sent him to see Mr. Mpelo, the Registrar of Societies for Zambia.

Mr. Mpelo took a liking to my husband and Don began witnessing to him. On one of the visits to his office while trying to register our church, Mr. Mpelo invited us to his home for a Bible study. After that visit, we soon traveled weekly for many months until a new work was started from those Bible studies.

One day I accompanied my husband to visit Mr. Mpelo's office, where he grabbed my arm, pulling me down the hall to meet one of his colleagues as my husband followed us. Mr. Mpelo said to his friend, "Here are some real Christians."

Mr. Mpelo patiently helped my husband with all the paperwork to register the United Pentecostal Church International for the first time in Zambia. What a blessing his friendship was to our church and registration was finally approved.

Flying Bullets

The trailblazer and Brother Sonkani had a big baptismal service on a Sunday afternoon. They had been teaching on Jesus' Name baptism. There was a large group to be baptized at the pond located at the edge of town. A great worship service was followed by the baptisms.

While everyone was worshipping the Lord, some came out of the water speaking in tongues. All of a sudden, bullets started flying in every direction and people ran to find a place to hide. It was chaos. No one knew what was happening. I frantically looked around for Kelli and could not find her.

Suddenly a loud, angry voice screamed into a megaphone, "Put up your hands and march forward towards the police vans!" We started marching to the vans with our hands in the air all the while hearing the angry policewoman yelling vulgarities. About that time, I saw Kelli climbing out of a large hole. She had fallen in with baby Gigi tied to her back. Kelli quickly joined us and Gigi's mother grabbed the baby to safety.

As our church group of 50-60 people approached the vans, we were told they were looking for my husband, myself, and a few of the leaders. My husband told Kelli to stay by our side. The police informed us we were being taken to the local police station. Believe me, we prayed earnestly as the van traveled to our destination. None knew why they wanted us. Once we were there, the police began questioning us, "Who are you? Where are you from? What are you doing in Zambia?"

Apparently, someone from the old opposition group had notified the police there were white South Africans at the pond holding illegal services. Since the police took them at their word, they raced to the pond to see if they could catch us.

During the more than three hours we were held at the police station, the entire group that had been at the baptism walked a very long distance to support us. While making their way, songs of praise were sung and drums were beat in thanks to God for those who had been baptized and filled with the Holy Ghost. After the crowd of 50-60 people arrived at the police station, they serenaded us with worship songs.

Our leaders tried to defend us. After a few hours, Kelli started moaning and complaining, "Mama, I'm hungry. I'm hungry." Several times she repeated this since she was always hungry. Kelli continued her request when, in frustration, the policeman, told her, "If you want food, your family will have to bring it to you!"

Kelli wailed and said, "What am I supposed to do? My family is here! I'm going to starve to death because the rest of my family is in America!" It was beginning to get dark when the officer in charge finally said, "You are free to go but I will keep your passports. Report here tomorrow morning at 8 o'clock."

At last we could go home after being held for more than three hours. We thanked our leaders and church group for their support and prayers and went home to spend the night in prayer.

Don, Kelli, and I returned the next morning to the police station where my husband asked to see the name or names of the ones who had charged us with being South Africans and holding illegal services. The police did not give us a name but our passports were returned, and they informed us we were not being held.

My husband asked to see the police chief who had been on duty the previous night. The policeman told him, "He was not on duty," even though we saw his name was on the wall board in front of us as being on duty the day before. We felt sure the opposition group was responsible for the false charges and still making threats to get us out of the country. It was a miracle no one was hurt. Once again, our God brought us through and the hand of the Lord was on His church.

Early Morning Attack

Early one morning around 3 o'clock, Don was kneeling in prayer in our living room. This was his usual private time to talk to God. Suddenly a very large rock smashed through our living room window just missing his head. The house was peppered with rocks and windows broken by two or three men in the yard. We heard them smash the windshield of our car. Scipio, our dog, got scared and ran off.

One of the men shouted to my husband, "Come outside!" He did not answer them. Quietly we prayed for God's protection. The vandals stayed out there until daybreak. Just before they left, a small fire was set under our car.

After we knew the vandals were gone, Don quickly went outside to see the damage and found the small fire still smoldering under the car and put it out. Borrowing a neighbor's phone later that morning, he called the police station to report the problem. The police told him they had no transportation and said, "If you will drive your car to the station, we can inspect the windshield. If you want them to check your house for damages, they will need a round-trip ride."

Don drove to the station and returned with the police. Once they checked the entire house, they told us nothing could be done since we lived outside the city limits.

The words of the psalmist took on real meaning for our family that morning. "The angel of the Lord encampeth round about them that fear him, and delivereth him" (Psalms 34:7).

A few days later, Scipio became very sick and died. Kelli was broken-hearted about losing her dog. Normally she slept in a bedroom at the back of the house. Since the vandals' visit, she nightly made a pallet in the hallway and slept that way for a long time before she was able to return to her own room, afraid the men would return.

By this time, we could say with Paul, "For a great door and effectual is open unto me, and there are many adversaries" (I Corinthians 16:9). The Lord opened the door for this truth to be in

Zambia. We were among adversaries but knew there would be revival and victory.

A Girl's Best Friend

Kelli started begging for another dog to take the place of Scipio, who had died. Her Dad took her to the local Society for the Prevention of Cruelty to Animals (SPCA) several times. Kelli liked all the dogs she saw and felt sorry for them. There was one very special dog, an Alsatian, similar to a German shepherd, that caught her eye. His owner had left the country and had not returned. The man who had been caring for the dog had run out of money to feed him and had brought the dog to the animal shelter to find a home.

There was a list of people who wanted this particular dog and had signed up for him before we did. The shelter waited another month to make sure his owner did not return. During that time, Kelli and her Dad visited every two or three days to see the Alsatian. The dog took to Kelli immediately and she brought him treats on each visit. One day when they were visiting the shelter again, the lady in charge told Kelli, "I am going to let you have the dog as he has really taken to you. I can see your bond with him."

Kelli was very happy to take her new large dog home (she named him Prince). They became best friends. Dogs were family pets in Zambia but also guard dogs.

When Kelli brought Prince home, Puddy, our cat, had just had six kittens that were only a couple of weeks old. Before we knew it, Prince grabbed the kittens shaking them. When he snatched one particular kitten, Puddy launched herself on his back fighting him like a lion. Kelli screamed and her Dad ran in and rescued the kittens.

Puddy finally calmed down enough to comfort her kittens. There was one little kitten Prince had shaken more than the others. Kelli felt it left the kitten retarded. Of course, she had to keep it and named him George. He became one of her best buddies. Prince got a stern reprimand from her Dad. Since he was a very smart dog, he knew he had done something wrong. Never again did he bother the kittens.

March for Victory

The trailblazer still visited the Lusaka city office to request a church plot four or five times a week but to no avail. This went on for a year. Supposedly the city had set aside 10-acre plots for churches. Each time my husband requested a plot, he was told, "We don't have any."

About this time, the Freemans came to visit enroute to South Africa. We told them a Bible school plot had been selected, yet permission had not been received to purchase or lease the land.

Brother Freeman asked my husband to see the plot. After driving the Freemans to see the land, they were well pleased with the location especially as it was close to town. Many of our church people had no transportation except traveling by foot. Brother Freeman felt the plot would be a good site for the Bible school and church building and insisted, "We need to march around this plot claiming it in the name of Jesus." All of us joined together marching around it, praising the Lord for giving us the land. In a day or two, the Freemans went on their way to South Africa.

The next week Don again visited the city office to ask for a 10-acre plot. The paperwork was signed and stamped. It was for a 99-year lease with an option to lease for another 99 years. When my husband arrived home, he was on cloud nine and we rejoiced all day.

Thirsty for Water

The chief of the Mataba area invited us to teach him about our message. This trip would require us to stay in the bush while using the chief's tent. Brother Sonkani was to join us on this trip. Since we would be gone a few days, we talked to Kelli. She wanted to stay with Mama Sonkani and the girls. Quickly she packed her things and went to stay with her friends.

Again, we were on the trail. The three of us took plenty of water with us since the weather was hot and services would be held outside. Once we turned off the main road, we drove many kilometers on an old dirt washboard road. When we finally arrived, three of our one-gallon water containers had holes in the bottom and the water had run out. Only two gallon containers were left but we felt there would be enough water for drinking if we were very careful. A little tent (with many holes) was set up on our arrival, to which we added our cots.

That night people began to arrive and sit around the camp fire, which was our only light. The trailblazer taught them late into the night because the people were so hungry for the Word. Everyone bedded down around the smoldering fire. We went to our tent which had been positioned a little ways from the fire to give us privacy. Thankfully, we had a flashlight to find our way.

Up early the next morning, we were brought heated water for bathing and were invited to breakfast with them. It was different but well prepared - roasted wild meat and yams with our tea. After breakfast, we had another service with worshipping and singing. A Bible study followed teaching the name of Jesus and one God.

Chief Mataba (as he was called) was a very nice man with a kind spirit. He came to the services asking Brother Sonkani to interpret, even though the chief spoke English well. Brother Sonkani also spoke his language. The chief's wife sat next to me for the three-day meetings.

The last water jug was going down little by little. My husband had planned a baptismal service for that Sunday afternoon. Once that was finished, the people would return to their different villages before nightfall. Since we could not travel at night, we needed to stay until Monday due to a gang of bandits who had been on the prowl nightly in that area.

Sunday morning we awoke to find our water jug empty and I was very thirsty. Service that morning was at our camp followed by a baptismal service, which was held a distance from us. It was a long hot walk and the chief and his family marched with us to the baptism while we sang and worshipped the Lord. Every step I could hear myself say, "I'm thirsty." It took at least twenty minutes to walk in the extreme African heat.

Once we got to the baptismal area, Don instructed the people to be baptized by saying, "Raise your hands and praise the Lord when you come out of the water." Baptizing 85 people took time. Many received the Holy Ghost in the water. We had an old-time Pentecostal baptismal service on that sweltering day.

By now it was past noon, the sun was scorching and I knew I was in trouble as my mouth was extremely dry and my lips cracked open. Knowing I needed water I thought, "I'll have water boiled when we get back to camp." Since I did not want to tell Don my condition, I kept quiet.

Finally we arrived back at camp. I lay down on my little cot but as the sun glared into the tent's many holes, I realized I needed God's help.

In a little while, Don came to our tent and told me he was going to take the chief and his wife back to their palace, as they called it, and wanted to know if I would like to ride along. I felt bad and told him, "I'm very hot so I think I'll stay at camp and rest." A few minutes later, I changed my mind because something urged me to go with him.

Sitting in the back seat of our pickup with the chief's wife, Don and the chief sat in the front. All at once, we turned a corner into the long driveway to their large hut, and saw a well in the yard. When Don slowed down, I jumped from the vehicle and ran to the well. I had never drawn water from a well before but I saw an old, rusty bucket tied on a long string. Grabbing it, I threw the bucket down the well and quickly brought up fresh clean water. Immediately I began drinking and drinking the cool water letting it drip all over me. It felt like life was coming back into my body because I was really dehydrated. Water truly is the source of life. "Blessed are they that hunger and thirst after righteousness, for they shall be filled" (Matthew 5:6). When we are really thirsty and desperate, God will fill us with that living water where we will never thirst again.

The trailblazer took us to Chief Mataba's area many times after that initial trip. What a blessing he was to help us translate some of our tracts into their language. On another trip, 145 people were baptized.

Leopard Hills

The International School in Lusaka still did not have a place for Kelli and the waiting list was two years. We had waited one year to find a school for her because she did not want to be home schooled.

About this time a new school year was to begin. In desperation, her Dad asked the headmaster of the International School if he knew of another school and he suggested Leopard Hills Secondary School.

Leopard Hills, a school of 120 children, was located a few kilometers out of town and not too far from where we lived. The headmaster told Don he would feel comfortable sending his boys there if there was no place for them at his school.

Her Dad took Kelli to the school and they accepted her after taking an exam. She was happy and excited about going to school but she was the only American. Most of the students were from African countries and one British girl. Several were the children of ambassadors. Kelli needed French lessons so we began searching for a tutor.

The Lord timed everything well. Kelli enrolled the same day as a girl from Italy. She did not know much English so Kelli told the headmaster she would help her in class. Lorenza was her name and she lived only a few streets from our home. Her father was a large petrol oil company's top man in the country. Kelli and Lorenza became good friends. It worked for us to carpool with her family. Don would take them to school and their driver would pick them up and return them home.

Brother Sonkani's oldest daughter, Ruthie, came to stay with us since Keith had gone to the states for high school. She was four years older than Kelli and was a good friend. This gave her someone to be with if we had to be away for a few hours, since it was not safe to be alone.

One day Ruthie came home to say there was a French teacher at her school and thought he would come and give lessons to Kelli. Don went to see him and the teacher agreed. This worked out well since my husband and I were frequently gone. Coming to our house eliminated the problem of getting Kelli to and from lessons.

The teacher was from Zaire and spoke excellent English and taught French, history, and math. He came to our house three afternoons a week. Mr. Nawazhi also helped Kelli catch up all her subjects she had missed for a year.

After a few weeks of Kelli's lessons, my husband started giving the young single French teacher Bible studies. The studies went on several weeks. Her teacher started coming to church and was filled with the Spirit and baptized.

Blocks and More Blocks

The first week of August 1982, my sister and her husband paid Keith's way home after finishing high school in the states. Their sacrificial gift was a large blessing to our family and to the work. It was so good to see him. No longer a boy, he had grown into a fine young man. What a blessing Keith would be to his Dad and the church's building project.

Sand was needed for the building program from a nearby quarry and had to be dug by hand. My husband hired young men from the church to help with the project. Peter, our yard boy, (really a young man) was Keith's right-hand man. Peter went everywhere with Keith and they became close friends. Keith was not allowed to drive alone because there were lots of car thefts in the country. Worse were the hijackings. Thieves would walk up to your car window with a gun and demand the keys and your money. If Keith, a young white man, drove alone, he would be open prey.

Peter rode with Keith to haul the cement which was used to make blocks. Thousands of hand-made blocks would be needed to fence the 10-acre church plot. Two to three men mixed the cement, sand, and water to form the blocks, one of them Benjamin Daka.

Daily Don bought cement as you could not leave unused cement at the plot because it would disappear during the night. One day when he went to buy more cement, the shop man said, "There is none. " Since the shop had no more cement, my husband located a plant quite a ways out of town. Weekdays one of our two drivers (Keith and his Dad) drove to the plant where they had cement but no sacks. If you wanted it, you had to shovel and bag it yourself. Thankfully, we were able to find sacks.

Keith and Peter made most of the daily trips to the cement plant, filled sacks, and brought it to the plot. By the time they arrived home each evening, Keith had turned cement gray. Peter had turned almost white or light gray. Filling bags was a slow process. Building the blocks one at a time was labor-intensive. Molded hand-packed blocks were laid on the ground to sun dry. Keith or his Dad hauled water in the back of our two-seater pickup each day to mix the cement. Building was slow but day by day we could see progress.

Witch Doctor

Brother Jack Leaman and his son, Rodney, were on a trip through part of Africa. My husband contacted him to come to Zambia as our guest speaker at the upcoming General Conference.

Preparations were made for our General Conference in Lusaka. Our empty plot was used for the meeting. Three to four hundred people were anticipated. The young men, Keith, and his Dad built a brush arbor for the services creating a shield from the hot summer sun. African toilets were installed. Unlike American toilets, each was a hole in the ground.

Brother Leaman and his son arrived just before conference time. This was always a very special time with most people camping around the plot. The nationals made little places to cook. A few stayed with family and friends. People came from around the country. God moved in a mighty way and several received the Holy Ghost and were baptized.

The greatest miracle to take place at our conference was what God did in the life of an old well-known Lusaka witch doctor. Many of our people had gone to him before coming into the church and being filled with the Holy Ghost. A witch doctor is a type of healer who treats ailments believed to be caused by witchcraft. Some of our church's young men had invited him to the conference, telling him there was a power greater than any he had ever known.

Lusaka's prominent witch doctor came to one of our evening services and sat in the back listening to the preaching. God's Spirit moved him very much during that service.

At the end of the preaching, Brother Leaman turned the altar call over to my husband. God moved on him to designate areas for people who wanted to repent for deliverance from drinking, smoking, and adultery. As he named the different kinds of sins, the trailblazer named witchcraft and pointed to the side of the altar. The old witch doctor made his way to this section where God mightily touched him and delivered him of many strange and evil spirits. Gloriously he was filled with the power of the Holy Ghost and later baptized. Following that service, the witch doctor weekly brought as many people as he could fit into his large blue dump truck to church.

Stamped Permit

One day Don finally asked, "Where else can I go to seek a water line permit for our Bible school?" The office sent him to the City Planning Department, a part of the city council where a permit was received to build the water line on the plot.

While my husband was there, he asked them about putting in electrical lines for the school but was refused permission. Don told them he had received an official stamp and signature of the city council board for the permit. The top man was called to speak to my husband. The man asked, "Who signed the permit?"

"You did," my husband replied.

The man said he had never signed a permit for us to be on that land. Since Don did not have the permit with him, he replied, "I will bring it in the morning." These were stressful times yet the Lord was there every step of the way.

Next day when the office opened, my husband returned with the signed permit. The top man came out to see him. Don presented the stamped paperwork on the land and the permit to him. The man's signature was on it (it was the largest signature on the paper). The man told Don, "Yes, it is my signature, but I've never seen these papers." After much talking, the man reluctantly relented and gave us the electrical permit. Again, God fought our battle and we were victorious.

Boom! Boom!

Finally, we had all the supplies to finish the Bible school fence. It was well on its way to completion. Work on the Bible school foundation was started. The plot was very rocky with huge boulders and large rocks scattered throughout. Larger ones were in the area where we wanted to build. Foundation work could only begin after the rocks were removed.

The trailblazer decided we needed a professional blasting company to remove the boulders and large rocks. Deep holes were jack hammered into the rocks so the blasting company could insert dynamite.

When the blasting company arrived, three men were brought to keep bystanders safely away from the blasts, with the help of our men. None of our youth nor villagers had ever seen blasting. The nearby public school was alerted to keep the children inside during the explosions. A few villagers and our young men knew about the project and were very excited.

All the village heard the first day's blasting because the high velocity explosives shattered rocks with a big boom. Windows and ground shook with each blast amidst dust and flying rocks everywhere. The sound was ear-shattering.

Villagers frantically ran to our property to see what was happening. The blasting company's security and our men kept the crowd at a safe distance; but they could not believe their eyes, and many stayed for hours. Others came on their way to get water and stayed awhile.

Huge boulders and rocks required a second day of blasting. Again, we had many curious onlookers. Finally, the school children were allowed to come to the plot after the blasting company trucks left. Foundation work could now begin.

Thieves in the Night

Electricity had been purchased for the plot from a neighboring public school. God had been working on our behalf; we were finally given permission to put in water and electrical lines.

Pipe was needed and a lot of it to bring water a long distance to our plot. Water was needed to mix cement for the foundation. Finding pipe was another problem. The Lord helped us find it piece by piece. The trailblazer and our young men started laying the water pipes. Each time we put them in, thieves dug them out overnight. He instructed the men to cement the main lines surrounding the plot.

Before the Bible school building construction began, Don had to make a trip to South Africa for construction supplies where he bought window and door frames, and electrical wiring. The electric company did not have any lines or poles to sell. He purchased the supplies and had them delivered. In Zambia, he bought what he could but not much was available. I remember him commenting cement nails were 90 American cents each. Cement sacks arrived in the country and cement was locally available.

When the supplies arrived from South Africa, guards were hired to nightly watch the Bible school plot. Yet, the thieves came to see what they could steal almost every night. Installed door frames or window frames were taken. Thieves broke the supply shed door, taking everything for their own purposes - trading or selling them on the black market.

Don asked for volunteers from the local church to sleep at the plot each night, hopefully deterring the thieves. Seven or eight men guarded nightly. Since there were no phones on the property the guards' defenses were ponga knives and whistles. If one guard heard anything, he would loudly blow his whistle. Other guards joined him blowing whistles and soon all the neighborhood dogs created an uproar which often discouraged the thieves.

Peter and other young men volunteered. Of course, Keith, wanted to volunteer. His Dad let him go often with Peter and would have gone every night if he could.

One night when my husband took Keith to the plot for guard duty, I felt uneasy about him staying. I even spoke to my husband about it, but he was sure everything would be okay.

In the early morning hours, a large gang of men came to raid the place. Our men had been doing double duty: construction work all day and guard duty at night. Keith was sound asleep on his cot when a guard alerted everyone by blowing loudly on his whistle. Some of the young men tried to quickly awaken Keith but he was a sound sleeper and difficult to arouse. All at once, one of the boys pushed Keith off his cot yelling, "Get up or you're going to die!" He jumped up and let out a big Indian war hoop, which was extremely loud in the night. All our young men ran and did not stop until they were at the nearby grade school.

Keith said, "Let's go back and run them off." Rocks were picked up and the young men started back towards the school, peppering the place with rocks. The gang left that night but they were successful in pulling out windows and window frames that had not been cemented well. Thank God for His protection over our young men.

Reserved Seats

Kelli was out of school for a short holiday and wanted to visit her friends, Peggy and Mavis, in Kitwe. Ruthie and Kelli were asked to come for a few days to stay in their large house close to town. A bus was required to make the trip.

Keith and his Dad placed the girls on the bus early so they could get there before dark. Don talked to the bus driver and asked him to keep an eye on the girls. Before the Lusaka driver left, Kelli told him, "Make sure you return for us on Sunday morning because I must be in school Monday morning." He wrote down her name and promised a bus would be there.

Word was sent to the Lumina family the girls were coming but the message did not arrive before they did. When the girls arrived, there was no one to meet them so they waited. Keith called Peggy's home several times but the calls did not get through. The girls waited the rest of the day but no one came for them.

When it was getting towards evening, Kelli told Ruthie they needed to get a hotel room for safety since it was not wise to stay at the bus yard and said, "I will book a room." About the time the girls were leaving to search for a room, Mr. Lumina arrived. He had just received the call from Keith and was very worried about the girls. God protected them that day and the girls had a great visit.

On Sunday morning, Mr. Lumina and his wife brought the girls to the bus station and waited with them. It was packed with travelers. Due to a petrol shortage, some buses were unable to run. The line waiting for the bus was long. There were not enough seats for everyone. Kelli and Ruthie prayed they would be able to get home for school.

The Lusaka bus arrived and it had a different driver. When the driver came into the bus station with a piece of paper in his hand, he called, "I am to pick up a Miss Kelli and her friend, Miss Ruthie." The girls had reserved seats behind him. This was a miracle because every time a bus driver opened his doors for passengers, there would be a small stampede with pushing and shoving to get a seat. Often passengers would bump others out of their seats. The driver had been told to keep an eye on the girls by the previous driver. Kelli and Ruthie arrived in time for school. God answered our prayers and kept the girls safe.

Car Fires

Our Lusaka days were filled with the old opposition group still working to remove us from the country, and became vicious in their efforts. We learned they had paid someone to put witchcraft under chairs at our services but nothing happened.

One day Don pulled up to the petrol station. When the attendant lifted the hood, he let out a loud holler and jumped back, as Zambians are very superstitious. On our engine were dead leaves and a dead snake. The attendant told my husband, "Someone is trying to bewitch you." Reaching under the hood, Don removed the dry leaves and snake. Even though the attendant was very scared, my husband was not afraid.

A few days later, our engine caught on fire when all of us were in the car. The kids and I jumped out, picked up dirt, and threw it on the engine putting out the fire. A few days later, the engine caught on fire again while driving on a nearby road. Jumping out of the car, we quickly scooped dirt, threw it on the flames and extinguished the fire.

Another day when we were on our way to town, the engine caught fire for the third time. Since Don was in heavy traffic, it took a few minutes before he pulled over. By the time we were able to put out the fire, some of the wires had been burned and we needed a mechanic. My husband called Brother Silas, one of our preachers, to come to help us since he knew some mechanical repairs. When he arrived, Don told him, "We will need some new wiring installed." Brother Silas went to town, purchased the new wires and installed them.

Our troubles continued a few days after the car fire. In the early hours of the morning, our outside toilet, that was built onto our garage, caught on fire. This was next to Peter's room, our yard boy. He awoke to flames shooting up one of his bedroom walls. Once he forced his way out the window, he ran around the house beating on all of our bedroom windows while screaming, "Fire! My toilet is on fire!"

Don threw on his clothes while saying, "Devil. You can burn all of our toilets but we are not leaving Zambia."

Whitewash

Finally, our Bible school was completed and security guards were hired to live on the Bible school property. It was time to invite our leaders to the dedication. The Scisms and the Urshans were invited as special guests.

Keith and Kelli wanted to paint the exterior of our house before our guests arrived. All the markets in town were checked for paint, but none was found.

An Indian shopkeeper told them he had whitewash but it was only to be used on the outside of the house. It would look clean and nice; but he warned they would be in trouble if we had a heavy rain. With no other paint in the country, whitewash was their only hope to make the outside of our house look better.

Whitewash was purchased and work began with help from Keith's friend, Peter. Together they painted the outside of the house. The painting was finished a few days before the arrival of our guests; they were very proud of it.

Large rain clouds rolled in the day before our guests arrived. It looked like we were going to have a big rain. Talk about praying. The kid's were earnestly praying the clouds would move on to the copperbelt because it would ruin their whitewash. The Lord heard their prayers and withheld the rain.

Dr. Matepa

Special guests arrived the day before the Lusaka Bible school dedication. Chairs were set up outside and guest chairs in the walkway. The church board had invited President Kenneth Kaunda, Zambia's first president, to attend. The president was an ordained Church of Scotland missionary and teacher. Since he was unable to attend, he sent one of his cabinet members, Dr. Matepa, who well represented the president.

Dr. Matepa arrived with his security entourage, newsmen, and professional sound equipment. Brother and Sister Urshan sang before Dr. Matepa spoke because he needed to leave early. Since there was no music accompaniment, Sister Urshan sang a cappella with all her heart. You could feel the presence of God sweep over the place. While sitting next to my husband, Dr. Matepa leaned over and asked, "What kind of church did you say this is?"

Don told him, "We are a United Pentecostal church." After the first song, Sister Urshan began singing another one and her husband joined her. The Urshans blessed us with their powerful harmony.

Dr. Matepa asked my husband again, "What kind of church is this?" Don replied, "A United Pentecostal church." After Dr. Matepa spoke, his men started taking down their speakers but he told his men that he was staying for the rest of the dedication and to leave the equipment for now. Dr. Matepa was touched that day by the Spirit of God. The dedication was a very special day for everybody and would long be remembered.

After the service, Dr. Matepa invited our board, my husband, Brother Urshan, and Brother Scism to come to his Lusaka office. Gladly they accepted his invitation. Not long after their visit, President Kaunda invited all Zambian church leaders, national leaders, and missionaries to the State House.

Special Invitation

The trailblazer, our national leaders, and all denominational church leaders met with President Kaunda, Zambia's leader. The president wanted to talk to the religious leaders because he was alarmed with the large amount of youth crimes such as petty theft, shoplifting, snatching purses, and other misdemeanors. Zambia's youth was deteriorating and he wanted to see a change. Young people were also dropping out of school, which was unheard of.

President Kaunda felt the Christian churches could help direct the youth and encouraged the pastors to motivate the young people to be honest, get good jobs, and finish their education. A small refreshment tent with cold beverages and snacks had been set up on the lawn. It was a very hot day and Cokes, Fanta, Sprite, and beer would help quench their thirst.

Following the president's speech, the attendees were dismissed for refreshments. The departure for cold drinks resembled a stampede. Most everyone ran to the tent where they fought over cold drinks, especially the beer. My husband and our national leaders watched in shock as many grabbed four or five drinks. Since there had been a drastic shortage of beverages in the country for months, this was an unexpected luxury. While President Kaunda drank a Fanta, he talked to the leaders about ways to help the country and its youth.

After a short session following the refreshments, the president invited the leaders for another session the following day. Once the session began, President Kaunda informed them, "I am very disappointed in most of you." He told them they had failed the youth in the country and churches had not helped with family problems. The president implied many leaders were after money instead of changing lives. In frustration, President Kaunda angrily said, "Maybe we would be wise to try communism!"

The president admonished the leaders about their drinking habits and loose morals and told them they were a bad example for the youth. He was right because Zambia had many ungodly church leaders. Following this session, my husband prayed God's church would become a beacon in Zambia.

Formal Wedding

Keith and Kelli were preparing to leave for the states. Before their departure, Peter, Keith's closest friend, was planning to marry his sweetheart, Jane.

A month before the wedding, one of the greatest blessings was sent in the form of a used clothing package from the states. A small man's black tuxedo was included in the care box. It was just Peter's size even though it was a tight fit which meant he could not gain any weight before the ceremony.

Kelli searched the care package and found a couple of dresses that could be remade into a bride and bridesmaid's dress. (Kelli was to be Jane's bridesmaid.) Since Kelli had a sewing machine, she ripped the seams of one dress and created a brand new dress perfect for a bride. A bridesmaid dress was designed and sewn from another dress.

With the find of the tuxedo and makings of two beautiful dresses, the decision was made to arrange a formal wedding. Typically, most Africans had never seen a formal wedding with tux and bridal gown because most nationals were married by a village chief. Everyone was extremely excited and wished to help with the special preparations.

Keith spent many hours designing and building a wooden wedding arch which he whitewashed. Fern, my sister, sent cake posts to stack layers and the topper. What was unique about the topper, was that it looked like our African bride and groom. It fit perfectly on the four-layer wedding cake, which was my first and only homemade wedding cake.

Kelli and Ruthie formed stunning bridal bouquets, and wrapped the arch with luscious hot pink bougainvillea from our yard. Kelli designed and made a bridal pillow on which Jane could kneel, and created a lovely hand-made bridal veil. Peter and Jane's very special formal wedding, the first of its kind in our church, turned out beautifully.

Miracle of the Tickets

It was summer time in the states and our children were booked to return for the Arizona camp meeting. This trip gave them a chance to see old friends and family. Following this visit, Kelli would travel to Rapid City, South Dakota to complete her last year of schooling at the Black Hills Christian Academy and Keith would travel to Houston, Texas to attend the Texas Bible College.

Don booked a reservation for our children well ahead of time but needed exit permits before paying for them. Keith's came by mail but Kelli's did not.

Driving to the ticket office the day of the scheduled flight, Don left Kelli and I there while he and Keith walked to the Immigration Office to see if Kelli's exit/reentry permit had been approved. At the ticket agent's office, I begged him to wait a few more minutes since the office was closing and the staff was anxious to go home for the weekend. Hopefully, their Dad would return in time with Kelli's signed permit.

At last, Don received Kelli's exit paperwork and quickly returned to the travel office. When the tickets were purchased, he realized they were issued only to England.

The airline travel agent told my husband Keith and Kelli were on standby to the states. We knew if they were unable to get on that flight, they would have to wait until Monday for the next flight into St. Louis, Missouri. That would require them to spend two nights in England, pay for food, and taxi fare. Keith turned to me and said, "Don't worry, Mama. We will take turns sleeping at the airport." That would not work as Keith slept like a log.

Keith and Kelli had one hundred dollars each, the amount Zambia allowed anyone to take out of the country. There was no choice but to put them on the plane later that night.

Calling someone in the states concerning our children's connections to the states had to wait until the next day. Don had Brother Judd's phone number at headquarters. That night we prayed and trusted the Lord our kids would make it safely to the states.

Next morning, my husband went to the post office to call Brother Judd. Don explained the flight situation and told him, "They could arrive on one or two dates, depending on flight availability."

Brother Judd responded by saying, "Don't worry, Brother Ikerd. I will personally meet their plane in St. Louis on both days if needed." Brother Judd told my husband he would make sure Keith and Kelli make their connection to Arizona, their final destination.

Arriving in England on time, the airline agent told our children they would not be able to get on standby due to a clerical error. The airlines made complimentary reservations for them at a nearby hotel due to their mistake. Next morning, Keith and Kelli returned to the airport to check the possibility of getting a seat that day to St. Louis, rather than waiting until the following day.

Keith asked the airline agent, "How much extra would it cost for us to fly out today?"

"One hundred dollars each," replied the agent. Keith quickly paid the fee, which left them broke. Brother Judd met them in St. Louis and helped them make the connection to Arizona. Thank God for His protection.

21 Pies

When Keith and Kelli landed in Phoenix, they visited their Grandma Ikerd. Afterwards, they were able to attend the Arizona camp meeting in Prescott, seeing many of their friends. God blessed Keith in a very special way in that camp meeting.

Traveling by bus, they visited their Grandpa Cox in Idaho. The rest of the summer went by fast. The last leg of their summer was a short visit to Grand Island, Nebraska where my mother organized a very special 21st birthday celebration. The entire church was invited to attend Keith's party. His grandmother had lovingly prepared an entire meal along with a very special dessert. Twenty-one homemade chocolate meringue pies were waiting for the birthday young man and the guests. Mother was known for her chocolate cream pies. Keith had a one-of-a-kind birthday. His Dad and I were very happy to know his special day was such a great one.

Malaria Strikes Again

The trailblazer was anxious to attend a minister's seminar in Kitwe to visit the new work Sister Lumina had opened in the city area before we were leaving for the states. Her husband's job had moved him there, which was Zambia's second largest city.

Don and I visited Brother Malanga, our pastor in a village located at the outskirts of Kitwe. Camp cots were packed to allow us to stay for a few days, which we would set up in the back of the church as it would be safer.

On Saturday morning, I awoke with a high fever. The brethren prayed for me and someone was sent to ask Sister Lumina, a registered nurse, to check on me late that afternoon. Once she saw me, she told my husband the fever was very high saying he should take me to her home where she could care for me.

Don drove me to her home and Sister Lumina put me to bed. He stayed with me while she went to the local hospital to see if a doctor would give her malaria medicine. The hospital did not have any medicine nor did they have a doctor. By now, I was very, very sick with chills added to the high fever. What I had was cerebral malaria - the most severe case with polio-like symptoms which drew my limbs against my body, pulling me into a fetal position, accompanied with lots of pain. There was nothing to do but pray and trust God. Soon I became delirious from the high fever and begged my husband to pray if God was finished with me, that He would take me.

Don and the Luminas took turns sitting with me around the clock for several days. Thank God for His healing touch. The fever subsided, my legs began going down where they belonged, and my arms straightened out. Little by little, my strength returned. I am so glad we know the Great Physician. Close to two weeks later, we returned home.

Mystery Lady

The Thackers arrived just in time to get their feet on the ground before we left for the states. What a great blessing it was to have them. Don and I left Zambia for deputation in the states where we planned to spend Christmas with our children. Arriving by plane in St. Louis, the weather was extremely cold; the plane's doors were frozen. Mechanics applied heat to the doors. After an hour, we were able to disembark. The Christmas holiday was wonderful spent with our children. We had greatly missed them.

Once again, the trailblazer and I were making our way across America covering many states while visiting churches. Don loved sharing stories letting people know what great things the Lord had done for us on the mission field.

That deputation brought many changes in our lives. Kelli graduated from Black Hills Christian Academy in June and was soon to be married. Preparing for a wedding, shopping for a wedding gown, and selecting bridesmaid's dresses was exciting. Kelli's wedding took place in September to Michael O'Neal, the pastor's son. It was special as our whole family was able to attend. Kelli's childhood friend, Kassie Keys from Safford, Arizona, flew to Rapid City, South Dakota to be her maid of honor and sang at the wedding. Both fathers officiated.

After the wedding, we started deputation again. Don had been experiencing pain in his back a few weeks. I thought it was from sitting and driving so much. Deciding to get a physical exam, one was scheduled in Beaumont, Texas.

The doctor requested x-rays which showed a large tumor growing on his kidneys. Needless to say, we were shocked at the result. A specialist's appointment was scheduled for the next week.

No one knew about my husband's tumor because we kept it to ourselves and made it a matter of prayer. A couple of days later, we ministered in two Sunday church services in Beaumont.

Sunday evening as my husband stood to speak, the Spirit of the Lord started moving in a powerful way. As he opened the Bible, suddenly a lady in the back of the church stood and gave tongues and interpretation. In the message she said, "I am the Lord that healeth thee" (Exodus 15:26).

The pastor jumped up and laid his hands on my husband's back exactly where the tumor was. The presence of the Lord came down in a mighty way while the congregation worshipped. After awhile, he resumed preaching.

At the end of the service, my husband asked the pastor, "Who was that lady? She looked and sounded like a Zambian." The pastor had sat behind the pulpit during the interpretation and had not seen her. The pastor replied, "We do not have a Zambian woman in our church."

Looking for the lady after church, my husband realized she was gone. Asking the ushers about her, they said, "We did not see her come or leave." No one knew her and no one had spoken to her.

On Tuesday morning following the Sunday service, we went to the specialist's office taking Don's x-rays. The doctor's office x-rayed him two or three times and ordered a CT scan. A large tumor was shown on the previous x-rays but the new x-rays and scan showed none. This time, the tumor was not there. God had miraculously healed him. "I am the Lord that healeth thee" (Exodus 15:26). We serve a God who is the healer of all diseases.

Excess Baggage

The next year we met at my sister's home in South Dakota for Thanksgiving and to say goodbye to Kelli and her husband, Michael. Since Kelli was expecting our first grandchild in March, I asked if she wanted me to wait for the birth and she replied, "You go with Daddy. I'll be okay."

Since we would return to Zambia from Houston, we drove Keith back to school. Deputation was completed. We were anxious to return home.

Brother and Sister Rivers came to our last Sunday service, the day we were to fly home. God moved in a very special way in that service. Tongues and interpretation were given saying, "You are going to a new land and a new people." This was puzzling because we never dreamed the Lord had other plans for us.

The Rivers went with us to check in for our flight. Our luggage was overloaded with 27 sport coats and extra things we were taking. A Pentecostal Louisiana shop owner had given us new sport coats and men's underwear since she was going out of business.

When I went to the counter, the agent told me there was no way we could take all the extra suitcases. I explained we were missionaries taking extra clothing to our people in Zambia. At last, she said, "You can take it for extra baggage but must pay for the extra weight." Air France wanted over $1,000 but we did not have that kind of money.

Extra boxes were given to us for the overage. Sister Rivers put things back in the suitcases as I took them out and she kept saying, "You will need that."

A long line behind us grew as I tried to decide what to do. Sweeping the floor was an African janitor who stopped and leaned on his broom and said to the clerk, "Can't you help this lady take these things to Africa?" She left to discuss it with her Air France supervisor. By this time, the line of people chimed in and asked the agent why they could not help me.

Upon the agent's return, the overage fee was reduced from $1,000 to $600. I counted out my money. Sister Rivers looked to see how much money she had, but we were still short. Shortly after that, the Air France's supervisor came out and said they would put the baggage on free of charge. People in line clapped their hands in excitement.

As we started to depart, we asked our friends to pray that the extra weight would get checked through to the new carrier in France. Next morning after we arrived in that country, we experienced a long layover for our flight to Zambia. Luggage was collected and taken to the counter. The two very large suitcases were still too heavy. The clerk told my husband, "You must pay for the overweight suitcases." Don explained that Air France had flown them free as they were filled with clothing for our national preachers. The agent finally agreed to put them on without charging us but told us she could not guarantee their safe arrival.

Late in the afternoon, the airport's loud speaker asked for Mr. and Mrs. Ekerd to come to the check-in counter. I asked Don, "Do you think they are looking for us?" He was unsure.

A while later, another loud speaker announcement called out, "Would Mr. and Mrs. Ekert please come to the check-in counter." Since it was not our name, we did not respond. Boarding the plane, an agent checked our tickets saying nothing to us. God gloriously sent us a miracle in the form of free luggage.

How wonderful it was to be back in Zambia after being gone so long. A special meeting was scheduled for all the pastors and their wives a week before Christmas. New sports coats and underwear were gift wrapped and ready to be presented to each pastor. How thrilled they were to receive new clothes and went home happy.

Life-Changing Phone Call

The Thackers had done a wonderful job caring for the work while we were gone. Just before we returned home, they found a house with a phone for their family. The only way you could get a phone in Zambia was to find a house with one already installed because the country was still recuperating from seven years of no new phone equipment.

In mid-January, Brother Thacker came to our gate to tell us headquarters had called and wanted my husband to call back right away. It was late in the afternoon in the states but we jumped into our car and dashed over to the their house to return Brother Scism's call.

Don dialed the number and Brother Scism answered immediately. You have to know my husband because as he listened and said, "I see. Yes. Yes. How long do I have to pray about it?"

When he hung up, I was very curious to know what they had discussed but I knew it best to wait until we were alone. An hour or so later, after visiting the Thackers, we left for home.

Once we were on our way, my husband said, "You will never guess what Brother Scism called about. He called to ask us to go to South Africa to bring the church together as apartheid was soon coming to an end."

Don told me he had had a dream in the early hours of the morning before Brother Thacker came to our gate. He said, "In the dream I was in a boat. Brother Judd came alongside me in another boat and said, 'Brother Ikerd, get in this boat. We need you.' " My husband told him he was happy in the boat. Again, Brother Judd told him he needed him. When Don awoke from the dream, Brother Thacker was at our gate. As we discussed this, we recalled the tongues and interpretation in Beaumont where God had said, "Soon you will go to a new land and a new people."

The trailblazer, informed headquarters we were willing to make this move if the South African church would accept us.

200+ more photos are available at the Facebook Page dedicated to The Trailblazer! Just search online and Like the page to see the entire catalogue of missionary adventure pictures that were not able to be printed here.

Don Ikerd as a young man

Don Ikerd in uniform, Yuma AZ.

Ikerd Family in Prescott, AZ.

Ikerd Family arrival in Kenya, Africa

Kenya Bible School and church complex with the Ikerds and Bro. And Sis. Harris

Bro. and Sis. Ikerd, Keith and Kelli in Kenya

Bro. Ikerd dedicating new church plot with Keith and Kelli

The Ikerd family

Bro. Urshan and Dr. Matepa Ribbon cutting in Lusaka

1977 Mufulira conference with Bro. Ikerd

Peter and Jane's wedding party in Lusaka

Bro. Ikerd with Bishop Mansaka and old Ndola church board

Zambia visit with Bro. Ikerd, Bro. Sonkani, pastor, and Bro. Jimmie Moses, West Zambia

1993 First National Conference where leader voted in as superintendent, Durban, South Africa

South Africa – Ministers with towels

South Africa Bible Institute ribbon cutting (R-L): Bro. Ikerd, Bro. Leaman, Bro. Dan, Bro. Makheti, Bro. Coetzee, student Janni Smith, Bro. Antonio, Sis. Coetzee

1991 South Africa's First Multiracial Conference in Johannesburg, South Africa L-R: Bro. Dan, Bro. Reddy, Bro. Ikerd

1991 Bro. Ikerd at First Multiracial Conference

Bro. And Sis. Ikerd

A Challenge of a Lifetime

The trailblazer and I arrived in South Africa on February 17, 1986 and quickly realized we had a lot to learn about the country.

Soon we were to understand why Brother Judd had said in my husband's dream, "We need you." South Africa's apartheid system enacted in 1948, was coming to an end. Don's help was needed to usher in a new united church governed by a South African board.

The trailblazer's assignment was to work with the four different groups of people to bring their churches together after apartheid. Four missionaries were responsible for each group. In 1950, all South Africans were required to be racially classified into one of these categories: Whites, Blacks, Coloreds, and Indians. The people of South Africa were divided by race and were forced to live apart from each other.

South African churches had been racially segregated but now needed to accept one another. This was difficult after almost 50 years of their government's enforcement of racial segregation.

Brother and Sister Charles Abernathy, one of the current missionaries in South Africa, met us at the airport; and we stayed with them a few weeks. Since they were soon departing for deputation in the states, we were able to lease their house.

Another missionary family, the Porters, would be leaving for the states for deputation. Before they left, they took us to meet Brother Mokheti, our Black superintendent. Brother Porter was in charge of the Bible school in Tembisa township. Their next appointment would be Swaziland.

Returning to our house from the Bible school, we had a message from my sister telling us our daughter, Kelli, had given birth to our first grandson, Michael Shane O'Neal. Becoming grandparents was a thrill.

Another missionary family, Brother and Sister Gary Abernathy, stayed until June when their boys got out of school. The Abernathys helped us meet many of our Colored pastors and saints in

Potchefstroom. They had done a great job working in the Cape and Johannesburg areas teaching Bible school classes. Soon they were on their way to the states for deputation. Malawi was their next missions appointment.

Now we found ourselves on our own in a strange land. We called Brother and Sister Clausen, our White superintendent, to arrange a visit with them. Several years before, we had met them when we attended a missionary retreat in their city. My husband told him we would love to come on Sunday to visit their church.

Brother Clausen graciously invited us for service in Pretoria with directions to get there. The service was in the Afrikaans language. Following the service, we visited the Clausens in their home next to the church. We were invited back the next week.

The decision was made to visit our Colored assistant superintendent while we were in Pretoria since he lived in Eersterust.

As promised, we returned to visit the Clausens on our way home and had a good visit with them. Brother Clausen shared with my husband the locations of the churches. Without his help, we would not have known how to locate them for future visits as the new missionary to South Africa was anxious to visit each one as soon as possible.

Don started visiting the churches in the Johannesburg and Pretoria areas. The first few months went by in a whirlwind of traveling and getting acquainted with the nearby churches, visiting the Jannie Smith and Monroe families. My husband taught and preached in their churches always followed by dinner and fellowship.

The trailblazer knew his responsibility to South Africa was to bring the churches together and felt this could be accomplished by getting them together for: meetings, fellowship, seminars, minister meetings, ladies meetings, youth meetings, Sunday School teacher meetings, and marriage seminars.

The saints in South Africa were well established in the Word with good leadership and wonderful missionaries who had done an excellent job training and teaching the pastors. Communication and relationships were needed now to bring the segregated churches together. My husband was a soft-spoken man with a wonderful sense of humor. God gave him a lot of wisdom to become the trailblazer in South Africa. This was not pioneering a church in a new area but pioneering the breakup of apartheid. There could not be unity until the churches came together which would require a lot of love, prayer, and fasting.

The trailblazer tried to help them see how the other groups felt by planting seeds of forgiveness, understanding, and above all, love towards the other race groups that took years to germinate. This took a lot of love and persistence on his part to see the dream come to fruition. Everyone had to learn to accept each other.

The Special AIMer

Keith came the last of June on the Associates in Missions (AIM) Program for nine months after graduating from Texas Bible School earlier that month. We were very happy to have him with us again. What a great blessing he would be to the youth, arriving in time for the European camp meeting. Keith helped with the special activities for the youth and did a wonderful job teaching.

The next month was the Colored's camp meeting at Humansdorp. The three of us stayed in a little place at nearby Jeffery's Bay, a place by the sea known for its surfing. The Lord blessed our camp meeting. Ten received the Holy Ghost and several were baptized.

The Colored district had built a huge building they used for services. A foundation had begun for a large dorm - one side for the girls and ladies and one side for boys and men. The dorm was to be used for large meetings and conferences.

Continuing on our trip, Keith helped his Dad drive to the Cape area. This time my husband wanted to spend more time with pastors, visiting their homes and little churches.

Cape Town is one of South Africa's unique attractions, filled with museums and old places to visit. South Africa's Cape coast attracts an estimated 800,000 local and international tourists each year to witness the Indian and Atlantic oceans splashing together at Cape Point, an hour's drive from Cape Town.

Our largest church building was in Cape Town where Brother and Sister Charles Abernathy had labored for years. All the little churches around that area came to the Manenberg church when we visited.

Henry, a young man in the Manenberg church loaned Keith his trumpet. While in South Africa, he taught himself to play it. Keith continues to play the trumpet to this day.

The trailblazer tried to always teach the ministers on Saturday followed by a big fellowship meeting on Sunday. Lunch was served followed by a Sunday afternoon service. The Cape's Coloreds had been blessed by good teaching. Most of the ministers and their wives had gone through the Bible school program. Once a quarter we tried to visit them.

There was a new church starting in the Mayfair area of Johannesburg where Brother Reddy pastored. The church was close to a large Indian market where you could find bargains from food and curios to blankets and plastic ware. What a lighthouse the new little church was to this Indian area because it was in darkness, void of the true light of Christ where people worshipped many different idols made of stone, wood or clay.

The trailblazer tried to plan each trip to visit as many pastors and churches as possible. The three of us traveled north to the Tzaneen area for services and celebrated Keith's 24th birthday by taking him to Kruger National Park.

A couple of months later, the Freemans, the Regional Field Supervisor of the continent of Africa, returned to South Africa with Brother Vince Kelley, a pastor and friend from California, who had come to make a film about Africa.

South Africa was to be the main part of the film, as the Freemans had labored there for many years. They had already traveled with Brother Kelley and filmed through East and West Africa where

Brother and Sister Freeman had ministered. The Freemans had been the first missionaries to South Africa, arriving in 1948 with their five children and were well loved and respected in the country.

Brother Freeman asked my husband to take them to Zululand to hear the Zulu people sing. Don and Keith were very happy to take them. Arriving late in the afternoon at the pastor's house, he did not know they were coming because he had no phone. Brother Freeman told him they wanted to film their Zulu choir. The Zulus were very talented and harmonized beautifully. About that time, a young man on a bicycle came by the house. The pastor sent him off on his bike to tell the people to come.

It was getting late by the time the choir members started arriving. Candles were used to sing by as there were no lights available. What a surprise it was to Brother Kelley that the choir needed no practice. The singing was truly anointed of God. He was blessed by their singing and later used it in the opening of the film, "Out of Darkness".

Many enjoyable days were spent at the old European campground as they worked on the movie. Keith and his Dad enjoyed this visit very much. It was a special time to be with their friends. It wasn't long until it was time for our son to return to the states. What a blessing he was because he had come at just the right time.

When we put Keith on the plane for the states, we did not realize all the changes that would come in his life in the next two years. While staying with my great Aunt Edna and great Uncle Jess Francis in Lodi, California, he met the Seagraves' family from Longview, Washington. In the months that followed, a friendship and then a courtship took place as Elizabeth June, the oldest daughter, became his sweetheart and wife. Don and I were very happy about our new daughter-in-law. Yet, the day of their wedding was a hard one for us because we were unable to attend due to our being in Botswana for special services.

First Multiracial Minister's Meeting

A committee was formed which was made up of the superintendents of the four groups in South Africa. The church committee agreed to follow the Constitution of the United Pentecostal Church International. The Executive Boards of each group worked to get all the ministers and their wives together in Bloemfontein for the very first time. The committee found a hotel in the middle of town that would accommodate all. A lot of teaching was done prior to this event to prepare the ministers for this special meeting. The meeting's theme was, "Let Us Rise and Build".

There was a real air of excitement among most of the preachers. This meeting was a milestone in their lives and in their country. The trailblazer knew he had to get the ministers and their wives together before he could get the people together. This was a great new beginning.

Leaving the day before the meeting in Bloemfontein, we stayed an extra night to get everything ready. Many of the Blacks, Coloreds, and Indians had never been to a hotel in a city. Their enthusiasm was very high. Most of the ministers had to arrange transportation. Since some could only come after work, people checked into the hotel at different times.

Don and I stayed up late to welcome everyone. When the Indians arrived from Durban and were registered, they all crowded into the hotel elevator. It stopped working and was stuck midway between the floors. Quickly it had become overloaded with too many people and too much luggage. The hotel owner came to check out the problem and became very upset. Don saw his anger and tried to diffuse the situation by saying, "One thing we just learned is we cannot put 16 people and their luggage in the lift at one time." The owner went to see what he could do to get the elevator moving to the next floor.

Women and most of the luggage were lifted through the ceiling opening to the next floor. Finally, the elevator started working with no more than eight people at a time. Oh, what an experience.

A banquet was scheduled for Saturday night. That afternoon following our ladies' classes, a very angry European pastor came to me and said, "You had better tell the ladies they cannot nurse their babies in public. They must take them outside." Typically in this country, non-Whites had always nursed their babies in the open with nothing covering themselves or the baby. While pointing his finger in my face he said, "You had better tell them or I will go into the ladies meetings and tell them."

There would be trouble if he told them, as angry as he was. Also, I knew the ladies would take it from me better than they would from him. By now another brother had stopped to tell me they would not put up with this type of nursing. I told both, "I will take care of it."

Silently praying the Lord would help me, I returned to the meeting informing the women it was not the White custom to nurse their babies in public and used the example of a visiting preacher from the states. The minister had experienced the public nursing in the church services and had told me, "Sister, I did not know where to look when this happens. Was I to look above their heads or at the ceiling?" He explained he was very embarrassed and his face turned very, very red. All the ladies had a good laugh and they promised they would take their babies out of service for nursing.

Everyone dressed up for our special banquet. There were beautiful flowers on each table. A European pastor's wife came over to me and said, "One of our Black sisters is nursing her baby at the table," insisting I tell her to take the baby out.

Looking around, I spotted the nursing mother, almost in front of the banquet table. Walking over to her, I put my arms around her and whispered in her ear, "Mama. You need to take the baby out to feed her." She replied, "I will. I'm sorry I forgot." I knew she had. She left, nursed her baby, and returned to the table. Remember, their culture had had many years nursing their babies in public. It would take some time for the mothers to relearn.

The meetings that followed the banquet were filled with situations that needed to be worked out and needed to find compromises. Hours were spent coming to an agreement.

One discussion was if the ladies had to wear a head doek (a head covering). This was an African custom. After many hours of discussion, the decision was made. The Black ladies could wear their head doek, but no one was required to do it.

Many customs had to be worked out that were not scriptural. Little by little, changes would need to be made that would strengthen the unity of the church as it came together into one church governed by one national board. Respect and honor had to be taught and applied by all. Each race had to trust the other race, as they would like to be trusted. I thank the Lord for His leading and instructing my husband.

As stated above, one issue to handle was the subject of ladies nursing their babies in church. Each of the four church groups had a different custom. In the beginning, there was no tolerance. No trying to see it from the other's point of view. One day after ten years of working on this, one person who had been most adamant about it, said to my husband, "We will just have to accept it as their way of life."

Another great barrier was their language differences. Some were determined to only use their own language. Through much prayer and teaching, they started using different languages.

Worship was another issue. Each group worshipped differently. Each began to acknowledge the different ways and be blessed by the others' worship.

Steadily the trailblazer worked on the groups' differences. Another issue was accepting all cultures into their churches. In time, they started making everyone welcome. This did not come naturally. But, by teaching and being examples, the pastors and churches began to make adjustments. Today you can truly see a beautifully blended church in South Africa.

All these needed changes would not take place overnight. South Africa's changes were similar to the early church when the Jews and

Gentiles had to learn to accept each other. In time, they became a powerful church reaching the world. What a mighty force they were. They were united by the Spirit of the Holy Ghost in their lives.

Even though changes had begun, there were still many walls to come down that had separated the church for years. Little by little, walls of resentment, lack of trust, and hatred began to crumble. Every trip the superintendents made seemed to strike a blow to the walls.

This special ministers' meeting at Bloemfontein bridged the way to new relationships among all cultures. Since this was the very first time all four groups ate together, each group's customs were addressed. Two groups used their fingers and hands. Another group used only a fork and knife to eat everything, even hamburgers. Another group used only a large spoon. Yet, they managed to eat together.

The Assignment

Each of the groups had a church board which had great men who loved this truth and had a desire for the church to grow and go forward. My husband's assignment had to become their assignment, their goals and ambitions. It would not work if it was just one man's ideas, hopes, and dreams. It had to be planted into the hearts of each board member in each group. My husband knew that prayer was the key to bring them together.

The trailblazer began visiting each of the men on the executive boards from each group knowing this would take time yet he set out to do just that. His one goal was to be a blessing and leave the pastor and his family spiritually stronger. Often he went to the main leaders over and over to plant the desire to become one church and one body in the land. Little by little he felt the walls coming down. In some areas of the country, the old apartheid system was unyielding. It is amazing what prayer and the Holy Ghost can do. In time, pastors and leaders were changed by the power of a living God.

Soon after this, the trailblazer decided to start traveling with the four superintendents to the different parts of the country. There had been some changes in leadership. Brother Clausen had stepped down. Brother Jannie Smith became the new White superintendent. Brother King resigned and Brother Antonio was voted in as the Colored superintendent. Brother Dan Ragavaloo was the Indian superintendent and Brother Elias Mokheti, the superintendent of the Blacks.

These trips became very costly. The four men were told instead of getting each man a room at a hotel or guest house, they needed to share rooms with twin beds so they could save money. My husband said he would share a room with Brother Mokheti, the Black superintendent and the oldest. What a great spirit he had. The other men teamed up. This paved the way for the church to come together and learn to work with another race. Real friendships developed from these times together.

Double Blessing

Brother Freeman asked my husband to help Sister Nix get settled into her new country, Bophuthatswana. The trailblazer and I traveled two or three times to that area to check out the country before Sister Nix arrived. A young lady by the name of Cindy, accompanied her. The four of us arrived late in the afternoon in Mafeking and began the process of driving up and down the streets to find an empty building that could be used for a church, and an empty house in a good area for her home.

After searching a couple of hours, we saw a nice old house that was empty. My husband stopped so we could look at the house. Sister Nix, Cindy, and I peeked into every window. Coming back to the car, we got in and began talking about the house. The car would not start. Don tried over and over yet the engine would not turn over and finally said, "Maybe you ladies could push it out of the drive and down the road to see if it would start."

The three of us got out of the car and pushed it but the car refused to start. It was now around 5:30 p.m. About this time, a European man came by on a motorcycle. He stopped and said, "I live in that corner house. You can push it into my yard and I'll help you take a look to see what is wrong."

After he saw our struggle trying to push the car, he helped push the car into the drive behind his house. He invited us into his house where his wife was cooking Sunday dinner. She was very kind and stopped to serve us juice on a tray. The man introduced himself as Mr. Thompson, telling us he was from Zimbabwe, formerly known as Rhodesia, and had served in the war but was now retired. The Thompsons insisted we stay for dinner.

By now, it was getting late. Mr. Thompson told Don he would take a look at the car after dinner. After eating, they went out to the car and tried to start the car. It started immediately, making us very happy. Once in the car, we looked for a guest house or hotel to spend the night.

Next morning we set off to find a building or a house. There did not seem to be any. Late in the afternoon, we found a building similar to a duplex. One side was used for storage. The other side was a doctor's office. Inside we saw the doctor who said the owner was a man who lived on Sheppard Avenue, and gave us the address and directions.

You can imagine how shocked we were to drive up to the front of the house where the Thompsons lived - the owner of the building. They were just as surprised to see us. Again, we arrived about dinner time. Don asked about the building. Mr. Thompson asked Sister Nix why she needed the building. She replied, "To hold church services."

He said, "Why don't you use the Memorable Order of Tin Hat (MOTH) building?"

Sister Nix replied, "We need to see the one in charge of the hall."

Mr. Thompson said, "I am that man."

While my husband and Sister Nix talked to him at length, they finally agreed the church would be the only one to use the hall. Mrs. Thompson again served us juice and the added treat of hot, homemade cookies. Afterwards, we returned home. What an answer to prayer.

The next week Sister Nix and I set off in search of an empty house and finally found one. She told me, "God impressed on me this house would be mine."

The neighbors told us they thought the house had been sold or rented the prior week. Returning to our hotel room, we prayed about it. We learned the house had been sold; the new owners had moved in. Somehow the buyer's funds did not clear. The owner called to tell us the house was Sister Nix's. God gave us a double miracle. Sister Nix had a place to live and a place for services.

New Territory

The trailblazer continued to travel with the four superintendents. There were many lessons along the way that were valuable to the men. The four superintendents received no pay for traveling but gave themselves to the work of God. All of them had one goal and one vision. That was to see their group come together in a united effort and to see revival in their land, that had been separated by many years of mistrust and bitterness. These four men were planting love and trust in a new multiracial church and were starting to see walls come down.

The committee, consisting of the four superintendents set up by my husband, had many board meetings. There were many late-night sessions debating and working out situations to fit all groups that would be equal and fair.

Brother Mokheti, the superintendent of the Blacks, invited us several times to go with him to a new area, Botshabelo, which was about one hour and twenty minutes from Bloemfontein. An appointment had been made so he could teach the preachers and churches in that area. Two or three pastors of Trinitarian churches were also invited. So many came to the meeting that two services were held outside.

One of the trinity pastors was an older woman who desired to be baptized in Jesus' name. The trailblazer traveled to her little church the following month to teach and baptize her and some of her people. The Lord had opened new doors in the area and we were thankful.

Our next visit was to a little town enroute to Botshabelo to visit a Colored family. The man's job had moved him to the area but there was no church. Arriving on Friday, we had service in their home. An appointment was made to stop back to see them on Sunday evening upon our return to Johannesburg.

The following Saturday morning we set off for our service with the lady pastor. Brother Mokheti and his wife had traveled a couple of days earlier to hold a service. There was a great move of God and many people desired to be baptized in Jesus' name.

The service was opened for testimonies and questions answered by my husband and Brother Mokheti. The elderly lady pastor got up to testify. Since she did not speak much English, Brother Mokheti translated. During the testimony, she pointed to my husband and repeatedly said, "I love this man." Brother Mokheti was embarrassed and turned red. At last, she stopped repeating it and said, "I love this man because he brought me truth." The lady pastor was truly happy to receive the Jesus' name message. Some months later, she passed away. Thank God he was able to share this great truth with her and her saints.

Bomb Scare

Brother Mokheti called my husband and asked if we could come to visit them in Tembisa, a high-risk area often with much unrest. The next Sunday morning we set off for the Tembisa township. Brother Mokheti had made arrangements to send a car to escort us into the township. When we arrived, we came upon a roadblock where a soldier asked "Where are you going? What are you doing?"

Don explained we were American missionaries. The young soldier was very nice but said, "Pastor, I am short-handed. If you run into any trouble, I will not be able to help you. You will be on your own."

The soldier advised us not to go and said, "You need to call your pastor and tell him you cannot come." Needless to say, the people were very disappointed.

After our return home, Brother and Sister Dan, our Indian superintendent, who lived in Durban, called to invite us to hold services and spend the night with them. We traveled five hours to get there. The next morning we rode to town with the Dans. We were so busy talking we did not notice anything going on around us. Brother Dan drove into a parking garage and parked. Once out of the car, we made our way to the elevator. Since the elevator was not working, we walked down the stairs. I had a strange feeling but brushed it off. When we got to the sidewalk, a young policeman looked up shocked to see us and said, "Run! Get away! There is a bomb in that building! We thought we had everyone out!"

I remember Brother Dan telling the young policeman when leaving his car, "It will be okay because the Lord will protect my car." Starting off in the direction he pointed, we left Brother Dan's car in the garage. After several hours, the bomb was found and defused allowing us to return and pick up the car. Later we learned the bomb was the largest ever found in Durban. God protected the car and us.

Spin Like a Top

Traveling to Cape Town the next week, the trailblazer decided to drive the coastal route from Durban to Cape Town where we were to attend a special board meeting. It was getting dark and we were trying to get to Cape Town before it was too late. Soon we realized we had to stop because it would be too dangerous. The first place we stopped did not take Whites. Apartheid took years for the country to accept, as it took years for the church to work through it.

On our way again, we needed to find a hotel. About 30 kilometers out of Cape Town, rain began to fall. All of a sudden, three drunk young men ran out in front of us. Don swerved to miss them but the highway was very wet. The car began to spin like a top and started going down the highway backwards. It dropped off the edge of the road rolling three times, breaking my seat and throwing my head and shoulders onto the back seat.

A car behind us stopped to see if they could help. The occupants were very surprised to see we were okay. Later I learned I had three broken ribs. Other than that, we were fine. One of the men found my unbroken glasses several feet from the car. The young men took us to the Holiday Inn because it would not be safe to stay alone on the roadside at night. They helped us call the breakdown man (tow truck). It was best for me to wait until morning to see a private doctor. After we arrived in our hotel room, we sat on the two beds looking at each other and began thanking God for His protection and mercy. Don felt he should call headquarters about the accident unaware it was a holiday in the states and no one would be there.

Don dialed the phone and listened as it rang and rang. Finally, Brother Judd answered the phone and said, "There is no one in the office but me." He just happened to be doing some extra work at the office.

Don told him what happened. When he finished explaining the accident, Brother Judd asked him, "How did you get this phone number? This is my private line."

He replied, "I called the main headquarters' phone number and you answered."

Somehow the Lord put him directly through to Brother Judd. After he hung up, he remembered he had forgotten to tell Brother Judd not to contact our daughter, Kelli, since she was one of our emergency contacts and felt he needed to call her so she would not worry about us. When he called, she was not at home.

After a few minutes, the breakdown man called to say he would come by to pick up Don to take him to the car. The man said, "Sir. There will be nothing left of your car. Any car left in that area will be stripped taking anything they can carry."

When they arrived at the car, it was just like we left it. Nothing was missing. Don's briefcase, camera, and checkbook were still there. The man walked around the car inspecting the damage. He asked, "How did your wife's seat break? It looks like your wife's seat broke throwing her into the back seat before the car ever hit the ground. If it had not broken, she would have been killed on impact."

The breakdown man told my husband, "How fortunate you are. The last car I towed in like yours the lady died." Truly the angel of the Lord was with us that day. God never slumbers.

After returning to the hotel, we sat down and talked about the miracle the Lord had done. As we undressed for bed, the phone rang. Don picked up the phone. Kelli, our daughter, was on the line. I heard him say, "How did you know we were in Cape Town at the Holiday Inn?" (We had never stayed there before.) Kelli had no way of knowing where we were or what room we were in.

Kelli said, "Daddy. I did not call you. When I got to my front door I heard the phone ringing and hurried to answer it. You were on the line."

Father and daughter had answered the ringing phone but they did not talk too long. Don inquired about the phone call at the hotel desk. No one had put it through to our room. Never were we charged for the call. Kelli never received a bill for the call. My husband said, "If I had known it was a free international call, I would have talked a lot longer."

A few days later, Brother and Sister Coetzee came to our hotel to take us to their home in Port Elizabeth about five hours away where we stayed at least a week to recuperate.

Miracle of miracles, our car was not totaled. It was able to be repaired even though Don thought it was a write off. The car was left for repairs and we flew home.

When our car was ready, Brother Jannie Smith flew with my husband to Cape Town to pick up the car and drive it home. While they were gone, I stayed with the Kings in Eersterust. The men ran into heavy rain on their way back to Johannesburg. The muffler fell off three times and had to be fixed. It was nice to finally have our car home. When I looked back at our accident, I saw God's mighty hand of protection on us.

Gang Goes to Church

The trailblazer was back on the road. Brother Mokheti called and invited him to visit his church in Tembisa. Brother Mokheti had to receive permission for us to visit the church from the powerful Tembisa gang leader.

Brother Mokheti had made plans for a car to meet us at the entrance of Tembisa the following Sunday. The car escorted us into the township. When we arrived, several gang members were standing outside the church. Some of church members escorted us into the building.

When the service started, you could tell everyone was uptight because of the gang members' presence also inside the church. The Lord came down with a sweet presence as we began to worship. Many were weeping and praising God. The gang members slipped away, one by one. The service lasted very long. Two or three church members rode in our car as we left. Other members rode in another car escorting us to the edge of Tembisa, and sent us on our way rejoicing in victory.

Shortly after this trip, the trailblazer decided to make a trip to the Eastern Cape where we visited our friends, the Coetzees. While there, we had Bible studies in the Colored area. Near the end of one of the Bible studies, two young policeman came in and sat down. After our service, my husband took time to visit them and invited the policemen back for a Bible study. One was very interested and returned for the next Bible study. God marvelously filled him and his wife with the Holy Ghost. God did a miracle in their lives and today they are pastoring a church in that area.

East London Arcade

After leaving the Eastern Cape, we were on our way to Durban. Along the way, we visited several areas. First we stopped in East London and stayed for a few days holding services. We met with Brother Scottie, the leader of the East London church and a member of the Black board. Always we enjoyed our visits with the churches. Brother Scottie planned a board meeting for Saturday and special services on Sunday for all the little churches in the area.

Don booked a guest house for us at the edge of East London since it was less expensive than the town center. Rather than staying by myself, Don wanted to take me into town the day of the board meeting. I told my husband I could write some letters, and wash my hair; but he did not want to leave me alone saying, "You can visit all the little trinket shops and get yourself some lunch. Then, go to the Holiday Inn and have afternoon tea. Wait for me in the lobby."

Always I was happy to visit the little shops and little arcades to spend the morning wandering from shop to shop. Soon I came to an arcade which had shops on each side and enjoyed looking for something new. Suddenly, I was very hungry. The hall corridor made a slight turn and there was a tea shop. Sitting down, I ordered a sandwich and tea. Needing to pass the time while waiting for my husband, I decided to write my Mom and sister a note. The waiter brought the tea and sandwich. I continued writing. When lunch was finished, the waiter came and took my dishes. While lost in my letter writing, I failed to notice the place was empty. Looking around and seeing no one, I decided to go to the hotel. When I went to the end of the little arcade, the gate was padlocked. Hurrying to the other end of the arcade, I saw that gate was closed with a large lock.

Quickly walking back through the arcade, no one was in sight. I was locked in. It was a Saturday afternoon and shops closed at 1 p.m. Several times I called out, "Anybody here? Again, no answer. Sitting down on a step by the gate nearest the street, I waited for someone to come by.

Two young ladies appeared. When I called out to them, they came across the street to the gate. I told them what had happened. One lady went to see if she could find a night watchman or someone who might be able to let me out. The other lady stayed outside the gate so I would not be alone. Upon returning, the woman said she could not find anyone.

By now, it was getting late in the afternoon. The three of us started calling out for help. A lady shop owner on the top floor of the arcade heard us and came to see what was wrong. Apparently, she had come back to pick up something that had been forgotten. I assumed she must have entered from the back of the arcade and did not need to come through the gate. Thank the Lord she had a key and could let me out. Once she found out I was walking to the hotel, she offered to take me. I was so happy to see my husband when he picked me up at the Holiday Inn later in the evening.

The trailblazer had had his own stressful day. The board meeting, being a trying one, had lasted a lot longer than he planned. Each person got to speak, which took quite awhile but they were finally able to resolve the problem. The service the next day was blessed and the little building was packed.

Swaziland Youth Visit

A guest speaker was coming to conduct special services for our youth. Since apartheid had not come to an end, we felt it would be best to keep the Swaziland youth at our home. Don talked to our neighbors to see if it would be okay with them if we housed 20 Black young people at our home, because we lived in an all-White area. Each neighbor gave us permission.

The next day we were gone for awhile. When we returned home, one neighbor had put his barbeque (called a braai) over the fence for us to use since he knew ours was too small for so many visitors.

The missionary, Brother Andy Carpenter, brought the young people for the special services. Their choir blessed our services with their beautiful harmony. Boys were to sleep in one part of the office and sitting room; girls were housed in the extra bedrooms. The young people brought their own blankets, making pallets on the floor. On Friday evening they arrived late. Their arrival was followed by dinner and a time of singing and devotion.

The next morning we were off to our services and did not return until late afternoon. The boys helped with the barbeque and the girls helped in the kitchen. That evening we had a wonderful time of singing and testimonies with the young people, returning home the next day.

Later in the day, we received a phone call from one of our neighbors. She said, "We want to thank you for showing us a great example of unity." They had truly enjoyed the youth singing and thought it was beautiful. Neighbors told us we were welcome to have groups or visitors at any time. Finally, we were breaking the barriers in our neighborhood.

Lord, Bring the Rain

It was conference time in Cape Town. Don invited Sister Nix, Cindy, and an AIM couple to go with us to the conference. Sister Nix's large church van was able to accommodate all of us and our luggage.

There were different farms in the Kalahari area that rented guest rooms or houses to travelers. It was hard to find one that would accommodate all of us, but I finally found one with two bedrooms and a sleeper couch.

When making our reservation, I told the farmer's wife we were missionaries and helpers. Arriving at sunset, she met us when we pulled into the farm. After we talked a little bit, she told us they were sheep farmers and in desperate need of rain. There had been none in over three years. She asked us to please pray for them to have rain.

When we arrived, their cook provided meat for a barbeque and supplied two or three salads and a dessert. Wood for our barbeque and food for breakfast were provided.

After our wonderful meal, we had a delicious South African dessert and tea, followed by a great time of fellowship. Before starting for bed, Don had everyone pray for rain. There were no clouds in the sky prior to going to our rooms. Some time in the early morning hours, we heard rain - a big rain - and it rained until daylight.

At breakfast, we were thrilled with the answer to prayer. When we were ready to leave, I took the money for our accommodations to the farmer's wife. As we were loading the van, she returned all the money and said, "Please keep the money and keep praying for our farm that we have more rain."

The Cape Town conference was mightily blessed of the Lord with a great outpouring of the Spirit. God poured out His spiritual rain just like He had poured out the physical rain at the Kalihari sheep farm. God had sent rain when there was not a cloud in the sky - a real miracle.

The three AIM workers loved their visit to Cape Town. They went home rejoicing.

Jingle Bell Christmas

Christmas was approaching. Holidays were always a hard time without our children since they were in the states and we were in South Africa.

The people of Cape Town invited us to come for their special services and to stay over for the Christmas holiday. For years they had told us how beautifully decorated the old town part of Cape Town was at Christmas. Sister Nix was invited to join us since her missionary helpers had returned to the states; she was alone. A place with two bedrooms was booked with kitchen facilities where we could prepare our Christmas dinner.

Early Christmas morning, Don and I knelt by the bed to pray. All at once, we heard a little boy's voice singing, "Jingle bells. Jingle bells. Jingle all the way." Then the little boy began humming as he apparently did not know the words. The song was repeated a few times and then his voice stopped. Right then I told my husband, "That sounds like Mikey, our grandson."

When we were up the next morning and ready to go, I asked the lady in the next unit to see if she had a little boy visiting her. She said she did not. I asked if she had heard a little boy singing early that morning. Neither the lady nor Sister Nix had heard the singing.

After Christmas, we returned to Johannesburg. When we arrived home, we called our daughter, Kelli, and told her about the little boy signing Jingle Bells on Christmas morning and said, "The little boy sounded like Mikey."

Kelli laughed and said, "Mama. He only knows a few words and then he hums the rest." We did not know who the little boy was, but we were so glad the Lord let us hear him on Christmas morning. It is always the special little things that God did for us that brought about blessings in our lives. We never forgot that Christmas.

World Trade Center

When we returned home from the conference in Cape Town, it was time to begin looking for a place for next year's conference. It would be our first multiracial conference scheduled to take place before the national elections for the new president of South Africa. The committee had been meeting quite some time about this conference. At the last meeting, they decided the committee would find a place in or near the Johannesburg area. Everyone made it a matter of prayer.

One day Brother Jannie Smith drove by the World Trade Center in Johannesburg. Afterwards, he talked to my husband about renting that facility for our first multiracial conference. Following their talk, the Lord impressed on Don in prayer to go to the World Trade Center, a very large center near the airport. The facility was used by big businesses and corporations for their conferences. My husband told the Lord there was no way we could afford that place, but the more he prayed for guidance, the stronger the Lord impressed on him to go to the World Trade Center.

After fasting and praying, my husband and Brother Jannie Smith decided to see how much it would cost for our conference. As they walked through the large facility, they knew it was way out of our price range and told the administration office they would think about it. Returning home, they prayed about it some more. The more my husband prayed and told the Lord there was no way we could afford it, the Lord continued to impress on his heart to go there. The duo went back to the Trade Center to talk to the man. It would cost a few thousand dollars. There was no way we could raise that kind of money. Knowing what God had told him, my husband booked it and paid the deposit to hold it for our conference.

Now the real test of faith came. Thankfully, it was several months before our conference. The men made a list of special people they wanted to invite and invitations were sent. There was still much work to be done. They proceeded with their plans.

Every single minister had to be contacted since most of our Blacks did not have post office boxes but used the nearest school. It would take time to get their mail because the school was closed for holidays in December, April, August, and other holidays.

Many did not have phones, and this was another setback. Invitations had to be mailed months in advance. The conference schedules had to be made up, giving each division equal amount of time to lead services and singing. This took an enormous amount of time and effort.

Conference meals were planned but there was the challenge of making menus to please all four groups of people. All of them ate different kinds of food. Whites ate European food somewhat similar to American food. The Indians ate all curry dishes, spicy food, and rice at every meal. The Blacks always ate mealy pop, a porridge made of corn meal and water, and cooked until it was a very stiff mush that could be picked up with hands. Some ate fish and some did not. Some ate pork but some would not. The committee worked out menus to please everyone. The World Trade Center was to prepare the meals, as that was the only way we could use their facility.

The trailblazer and I spent days looking for accommodations for everyone. The Blacks had previously stayed at the conference location with pallets on the floor or stayed with family or friends. The Whites and Coloreds had stayed at their own campgrounds. The Indians had never had to worry about accommodations because their conferences had been in towns within driving distance from their homes.

Conference registration was new to our people. Some had never stayed where they had to pay for lodging. Many would come by bus. We kept busy trying to find suitable places for all. Some would be accommodated at the Formula 1 Hotel and others at a campsite at the outer edge of Johannesburg which was quite a distance from the World Trade Center. The entire campsite was booked for our people. We prayed there would be enough room for everyone. Many would share the little campsites: six men and boys in some; six women and girls in others. So many would come that each campsite would be packed. Buses would drive them to the conference early in the morning and return that evening to pick them up.

Large ablution blocks were in the public area buildings with facilities for washing and toilets. It was the best we could do for the price.

Now came the task of visiting and explaining how the registration worked. Each division's board members were responsible to brief their pastors and churches on the new way of doing things and explain the expenses, wanting everyone to be prepared to pay for the lodging.

In a country as large as South Africa, it took time to get to all the different areas. All but one board member had full-time jobs and pastored churches. This was a very big undertaking and they did an excellent job getting the message out. Hard feelings or misunderstandings about this memorable event in the history of the South African church could not take place.

The months passed by fast. Time was getting close for our General Conference. One day I picked up the newspaper and read that the Convention for a Democratic South Africa (CODESA), a South African Convention made up of all political parties, was going to have their meeting in the World Trade Center on the same dates our conference was booked. Don was on a trip with the committee, but he had heard the news before returning home.

The balance on the Trade Center reservation had yet to be paid. After showing the newspaper article to my husband, he said he planned to go to the Trade Center office with Brother Jannie Smith. The duo prayed earnestly that night and went to the office early the next morning to see the manager. After talking to him, he said, "I can do nothing about it." The government had told him they wanted to use it for their convention.

Don asked the manager to talk to the group, let them know we had booked the place months in advance, and had paid the deposit. Brother Smith and my husband were to check back in a few days to see if he was able to work it out. With only a few weeks until our conference, how were we going to get all of our pastors and saints notified of any changes since they had no phones or post office boxes?

The church went to prayer. The men returned to the World Trade Center office later in the week where the manager had been told by the government to have our church book another place. Don explained to the manager our problem and told him there was no way we could change our venue on such a short notice. The manager finally said, "If you are willing, there is a large warehouse that is empty on the grounds. I will arrange it to look like a conference, putting in chairs and a platform at no extra charge."

The cost was now one we could afford. What an answer to prayer. The manager draped the warehouse with beautiful white and royal blue material, with the promised platform and seats. Also, we had the same security that CODESA had, which was a tremendous answer to prayer. The Lord had put us at the World Trade Center where we would be safe and easy to find.

Guests from the states arrived a few days before the conference. How nice it was to have a time of fellowship with the Ewings and the Urshans in our home before the conference started.

Don and I went early to welcome the ministers, their wives, saints, and invited guests. There was an air of excitement as everyone began arriving by bus, kombi, or car. You could feel the Lord in our midst. "I will walk among you, and will be your God, and ye shall be my people" (Leviticus 26:12).

First Multiracial Conference

On December 20, 1991 our historical three-day conference began. This was the first multiracial General Conference of the United Pentecostal Church International of South Africa. It was held at Johannesburg's World Trade Center. The church was three years ahead of the country's special election to end apartheid and was setting a precedent for the country.

The service with several hundred people in attendance began with Brother Murrell Ewing blessing us with his singing. When he began singing, everyone felt a strain. Remember, this was the very first time the four race groups of pastors and their saints met together. Slowly, the entire congregation began to worship. Walls of differences started coming down. Some wept. Some rejoiced. All were moved on by the Holy Spirit in a most unusual way. You could feel the presence of God pulling everyone together as only the Spirit can, making us one. The groups had been separated by invisible walls for at least forty-seven years. All of their lives they had been subjected to a system they did not make.

That first service was powerful. God started healing wounds. We saw a real spirit of togetherness. Following the sermon, everyone had a great time around the altar worshiping the Lord.

Up early the next day, we arrived at the morning service. That day would hold new challenges and victories for us and the church. Still, we had the hurdle of serving the food. The conference center catered the lunch and evening meals. By dinner time, we had complaints. Apparently there were some who took all the desserts not leaving any for people at the end of the line. My husband sent me to find out what happened.

Most of our people had never seen such fancy desserts in their lives. Of course, they wanted to taste each one. Some of the people came to me to sort out the problem and I realized at once what was wrong.

One young man said to me, "Mama. We only have one of each." I tried to explain to the whole line to take only one, not one of each kind. Since they had not yet touched their desserts, I went along the line removing the extra desserts. When they made up their minds which one they wanted to keep, there was no problem. Thankfully, no one was upset. All of them knew I was not being partial. After the problem was solved, someone told me. "Only you could have done that and not had any trouble." A valuable lesson was learned that day - to offer one type of dessert at a time until it was gone. Then we could offer a different one until all four types of dessert were served.

The evening service was greatly anointed of the Lord. Everybody was blessed again with the wonderful singing of Brother Ewing. That evening I sat near the front. An old black brother requested to sit next to me so he could better hear the singing. After listening to Brother Ewing sing awhile, he said to me," Oh, we have our own Jimmie Swaggart." Many of the nationals listened to Christian music on the radio stations and he was a well-known singer to them. What a blessing Brother Ewing's music was at this landmark conference, as it ministered to everyone.

A very special service was planned that evening. Brother Urshan set a precedent when he had Brother Hughes present monogrammed towels to the executive committee members and my husband, the new interim superintendent. He exhorted them on servanthood as their ministry was to serve the people. These men from that day forward were commissioned to be servants, just as Jesus had served his disciples. They were to serve each other and the church. That was the most moving and historical part of the conference.

The next day, two well-dressed European men came to our services. The Lord moved in a mighty way. Everyone worshipped and praised the Lord. The two visitors stood and then sat in the back of the room for a little while.

The State President of South Africa, F. W. de Klerk, was having a meeting at the World Trade Center with different political parties, during the time of our conference. The purpose of their meeting was to work on plans to bring South Africa together, and to work with Nelson Mandela to successfully end the country's apartheid system of racial segregation which would take a few years.

President de Klerk had heard there was a church meeting on the same grounds holding their very first multiracial conference. He sent the two men to check to make sure that what he had heard was correct, wanting to learn if it was really a multiracial meeting. (Later, we learned the two men were members of Parliament.) Apparently the men had reported their findings. A few minutes later, a messenger came with an invitation to meet with the State President. He wanted to see the people with the banner: "One Lord, One Faith, One Baptism, One Church, One God".

My husband sent word to the hotel asking Brother Urshan to please come quickly to go with them to this very special meeting. The president was delayed seeing our men by several minutes which gave enough time for Brother Urshan to arrive.

The trailblazer took our special American guests - Brother Urshan, Brother Scism, Brother Ewing, Brother Hughes, and the executive board members to the meeting. The State President was well pleased that we were there on the grounds accomplishing what they hoped to do at their meeting.

The president spoke at length with Brother Urshan about the church and asked him to have our church pray for peace in the country, saying they anticipated trouble during the upcoming elections. Brother Urshan told the President our worldwide church would pray for peace in South Africa and a safe and harmonious election. It was a wonderful experience for our brethren. They realized the hand of God had truly led them to this time in the history of the church. The scripture in Psalms 32:8 came to take on a whole new meaning for the church of South Africa. "I will instruct thee and teach thee in the way which thou shalt go: I will guide thee with mine eye."

The historical conference came to an end all too soon. Everyone loaded their buses and different kinds of transportation to return to their homes around the country. Don and I said farewell to each busload.

As I boarded the bus to the Durban area to say goodbye to everyone before they departed, I was met with some very disgruntled people. Someone had been talking to them saying the others had been favored. The Indians did not get their curry at every meal, as was their custom. I tried to explain. No group had ever eaten different foods. It was easier for some than for others. Some said they would not come back to another conference. When my husband boarded the bus and heard the comments, he explained no one was favored and told them the four superintendents had been in the meeting where the menus were discussed. Menus had been made and voted on by all the superintendents. Some of people began to cry after he explained this to the group, because they could now see no one had been neglected in any way. Unity is what we were striving for. Everyone had to be willing to come to a compromise. It was not like the old days where there was only one nationality to be considered. Now, all the churches had to be considered. Spirits were changed. Everyone returned to the next conference.

Breaking Barriers

The trailblazer set forth again with a new passion and vigor after being installed as the Interim Superintendent. The history-making conference did a lot to unite the church. In the days ahead, we saw the Lord not only watching over His church in that land, but watching over the country as it moved forward together making political changes. That would help to bring about a united country.

Now was the time to plan more meetings where the entire church could come together. Don embarked on a plan to invite special speakers, Youth on Missions trips, and the A Team crusades (a group of ministers who paid their way to come and assist with the crusades). Arrangements were made and Brother Treadway from Texas was invited to come for our very first multiracial crusade in the Transvaal area of Johannesburg.

The first night of the crusade I sat about three or four rows from the front. People came, but they still sat with their own groups. A large group of Whites came in and sat in the second row. Others came in and sat by them.

The Coloreds and Blacks got up to march around the front singing and worshipping as the main service began. Most of the Whites were not used to this type of worship as they were always more reserved, but just as sincere. They watched the others worship.

One young man punched his neighbor to let him know that they should join the worship in the front. The next one punched his neighbor on the shoulder, and this continued down the line. The first young man got up and went to the front. The rest of them did the same. Before long, they were worshipping just like the others. This crusade broke down more walls that had been barriers for generations and everyone could feel it.

The trailblazer left again trying to strengthen the new South African baby church. Don and I traveled from district to district and church to church seeing and feeling the new changes.

Don made arrangements with Brother Mokheti and his wife to meet us at a pastor's home in another area where we had a Bible study on Saturday afternoon. Following the service, we planned to get a room in the little town's hotel so we could be close to the church for Sunday service. Afterwards, we were invited to stay for dinner at the pastor's home where there was much talking in their language. Brother Mokethi said to my husband, "They want you to stay in their home tonight, and have bought new bed covers, pillows, and towels."

Brother Ikerd told him, "We would be happy to stay."

The whole village came by to greet us and to thank us for visiting their area. The visit made much news in that village because it was highly unusual for White people to stay in a black man's home.

Next day the little church was packed. God moved on many hearts and His Spirit was poured out. This visit was like Peter and the brothers visiting Cornelius' house in the Bible which effected his entire family. Believe me. The visit to the pastor's home effected the whole village and walls kept tumbling down.

The trailblazer started teaching seminars in every area of the country for ministers, their wives, youth leaders, and Sunday School teachers. One of the meetings was in the Cowtan area where we had a great mixture of races. The Lord came down in such a powerful way. A very large demonstrative young African man worshipped in the front of the church. The place was packed. There was no room for him to run while shouting as was his usual custom. He got up and started down the aisle. A young white minister and his wife were sitting in the back, with their toddlers on a blanket beside them. All of a sudden, the young man came down the aisle in a rush and shouting with all his might. His eyes were closed and both arms raised in praise. The couple tried to move their babies but there was no time.

The entire room was in shock. Everyone knew if he came down on those babies with his big feet, they would be hurt or even worse. You could hear a loud collective gasp from the people. When he was right at their blanket, he made a high jump in the air, clearing both babies while shouting and praising the Lord. All knew it had to be the Lord as he never opened his eyes.

There were many unusual things that happened during the seminars, youth meetings, ladies meetings, and area meetings. A big adjustment was the time factor. One group was very time conscious. The others were always late. A way to solve this problem was to set a time schedule and keep it. Don told everyone who was in charge of the services to start on time. When the people realized the services or functions would start on time, they began to come on time. No one wanted to miss any services or functions. Old habits began to change to new ones.

The length of services was another adjustment. Some loved to hold longer services because it was so hard for them to come since many walked a long way. With some adjustments, the ones who had been used to short services began to enjoy the longer worship. Everyone went home blessed. If people needed to leave before the service ended, they did. Many learned to stay longer. Don helped the ones used to a longer service to make them shorter by having only one speaker.

The trailblazer and the four superintendents continued making trips to different areas to strengthen the newly-formed baby church. These trips were always profitable as the ministers and saints became better acquainted with their new leaders. The leaders were men of God who had preached for years yet as individuals they did not personally know each other. These meetings did more to stabilize the new church than anything. Apartheid had created walls dividing the groups.

First Multiracial Ladies Conference

Don and I were working on arrangements for our first multiracial Ladies Conference. The ladies asked to have a special speaker from the states. We talked about it, fasted, and prayed for direction. Afterwards, my husband felt impressed to invite our old friends, Brother and Sister Daryl Rash. They accepted.

Since South Africa is so big, the 1993 Ladies Conference was held in three main areas of the country. One was to be held in Benoni, a suburb of the Johannesburg area. The Benoni church, pastored by Brother Princeloo, Sr., was large enough to accommodate us with kitchen facilities. The second conference was arranged in Sparks Estate, pastored by Brother D. Blaire, followed by the last one in Cape Town, pastored by Brother Patrick Chikwata.

Sister Rash would speak at our three Ladies Conferences while Brother Rash would speak at seminars for ministers and leaders in the three areas.

Brother Rash was asked to talk to all our ministers and leaders about opening a new full-time Bible school in South Africa for all the races. It would be the first of its kind and would need dormitories. Don believed Bible school training was the answer to reaching our nation with this great message of truth. He realized we needed to equip our ministers and leaders for the future as trained leadership was the only way to have and keep unity in the churches around the country.

The theme of the Ladies Conferences was "Let's Join Hands". Ladies came from all around the Johannesburg area and stayed with friends or family. Sister Rash did a great job of relating to the different cultures of ladies that were present, using Jeremiah 32:39-41 as her speaking scriptures. The beautiful verses that stood out were 39 and part of 40. "I will give them one heart, one way, that they may fear me forever, for the good of them, and their children after them. And I will make an everlasting covenant with them, that I will not turn away from them ...".

On returning home after the first conference, Don took the Rashs to Kruger National Park. He felt everyone who came to South Africa should see game in their natural habitat. This was a special treat for our guests. Reservations were made to stay at Satara Rest Camp in Kruger National Park.

The next day Don drove us into the park. It had been raining several days. As we drove, the car became stuck in mud. The three of us vacated the car and pushed it out of the mud hole. All park visitors were told not to get out of their cars due to the wild animals. This was an area where we could usually see lions. There was no choice but to get out and get the car moving. Later in the day we came upon a lion kill. A dead giraffe's legs had been left in the road. Apparently the lions had had their fill and had gone to lay in the shade, leaving the carcass to the jackals and vultures. Thankfully, there was not a lion in sight. Memories were made on that trip.

The second Ladies Conference was in Sparks Estate in Durban. The Lord blessed us in a very special way. As we sang and worshipped, it reminded me of how Miriam led the women of Israel with singing and dancing. "And Miriam the prophetess, the sister of Aaron, took a timbrel in her hand; and all the women went out after her with timbrels and with dances" (Exodus 15:20). What a beautiful sight it was to see the ladies at that conference holding hands, singing, and worshipping God in unity.

Sister Rash had an unusual experience at the Durban banquet. The food was prepared by the ladies in the church. Several food items were brought to her to see if she would like them. While looking at a beautiful pyramid of blue, pink, and red gelatin, she selected one of each color since she loved Jell-O. When she saw the ladies looking at her and talking excitedly, she stopped eating. One lady came up to her and said, "You're eating the decorations." Everyone had a good laugh.

In our third Ladies Conference held in the main church in the Manenberg area of Cape Town, God mightily moved during the services. Ladies from Eastern and Western Cape came together and held hands singing, "The Church is Moving On," and worshiping the Lord. God did a work in the mind and hearts of those women.

On our last Sunday in Cape Town, Don took the Rashs for a ride to view the ocean. Quietly he continued driving while making wrong turns. Sister Rash and I continued talking and watching for the ocean. Finally, after about one hour's drive, Don pulled off at an exit and said, "This is what I've been looking for." It turned out to be a 7/11 store. All of us laughed so hard because we knew that it was not what he was looking for. Sister Rash said, "Well, since we're here, let's go in and buy a snack." The four of us laughed about that for many years. What a blessing Sister Rash was at our conferences. Brother Rash left a big impact on our ministers with his anointed teaching.

First South African National Superintendent

After our return home, work began on the General Conference to be held December 17-19, 1993. The next few months were filled with traveling, teaching, drawing the churches closer together, and planting seeds in the hearts of the ministers and saints everywhere. It was getting close to the time for the church to vote on their own South African superintendent and a new combined multiracial board.

Don gave the licensed ministers instructions on the method of voting as he traveled from area to area. To be able to vote, licensed ministers had to agree with the church's Constitution. This was new to some of them and a learning process. He told them they would need to move to one side of the room during the voting if they were not eligible. All agreed.

The voting was scheduled for Saturday, December 18, 1993 in Durban. At this conference, a new United Pentecostal Church of South Africa was born with the election of the new national board. The theme of the conference was unity and becoming one (Ezekiel 37:19).

Brother James Kilgore and Brother Murrell Ewing ministered in this conference. The Freemans and the Hughes also attended. Many visitors came for this great historical meeting. When Brother Kilgore arrived, he asked my husband if he foresaw any problems in the voting. He said, "No." Don told him he had instructed the licensed ministers throughout his many visits to each area.

Brother Kilgore asked, "Do you think they will move to the side if they do not vote?"

Don answered, "Yes." This was possible only because my husband had well prepared them.

The trailblazer conducted the voting business meeting. Brother Kilgore was there to oversee the meeting. My husband received a phone call from me during the meeting. Quietly he answered the phone and returned to the meeting, never letting anything upset him.

Don asked this question to everyone in the room, "Who would like to be the next superintendent? Raise your hands if you want to be." My husband had a great sense of humor. It often came in handy at an awkward time. This was a crucial time in the history of South Africa. The decisions of that voting would affect the church in the years ahead. There were no problems as my husband predicted.

The unified United Pentecostal Church of South Africa was born with the newly elected national board. Brother Dan Ragavaloo, the former Indian superintendent for many years, was voted in as the first national superintendent of the newly-formed church.

A newly formed multiracial board was voted in. Our special guests prayed God's blessing on the board members and their wives. It was a beautiful service with a mighty outpouring of God's Spirit. This was a very historical meeting because they saw their countrymen voted in.

Afterwards, Brother Kilgore told my husband he could not believe how smoothly the voting took place. This meeting was a big milestone for the church. Some were worried about the future of the church but God had His hand on it. He alone saw into the future and paved the way for victory and unity. The church of South Africa was surely moving on, in one mind and one accord.

Landmark Bible School

Now was the time for Don and the leaders to go forward with plans for the first United Pentecostal Church International multiracial Bible school, one of the first in the country. It was to be named the South Africa Bible Institute (SABI). The Bible school was a new endeavor for the church of South Africa. The board spent hours working on the plans for the new school.

Time was needed to look at different venues to find one that would accommodate everything we needed. The brothers voted to use the old Pelindaba European campground, which already had dorms and a couple of apartments. The board decided they would open a church in the old tabernacle on the Pelindaba campgrounds. The students could have their church services and open it to the community.

Everyone was excited about the Bible school opening. That year was filled with traveling and recruiting students for the new Bible school. Men worked getting the dorms and classrooms ready. It was a full-time job coordinating these efforts as it was a large undertaking. There were many board meetings to work out all the little problems.

The trailblazer was able to plant a desire to see revival in their nation. God spoke to young men from Zululand, Johannesburg, Cape Town, and the Durban area to come to the Bible school.

The most important decision of all was to find the right man to oversee the new Bible school. This was the board's greatest concern. They began to seek God for His direction. South Africa had many towns and villages with no churches. The church could travel into the new areas by training men to open new works.

Don felt Brother Coetzee should be the man. All the board was in favor of Brother Coetzee heading the Bible school. He was a good teacher and a man of strong principles. The board quickly approved him.

After much prayer, Brother and Sister Coetzee agreed to come. Brother Coetzee resigned his church in Port Elizabeth as he felt the Lord directing him into full-time ministry training Bible school students. He also resigned his job from the police force. Sister Coetzee had a good job and was able to transfer, and so they moved to the Pelindaba campground.

One thing for sure, you had to have a call of God on your life to come to Pelindaba. It was in the middle of nowhere with only a few houses and small farms. There were no shops near enough to walk. No bus nor taxi services were available.

The Coetzees moved into the large apartment at the school across from the kitchen. Here they could keep an eye on everything. Remodeling had to be done to the dorms before the students arrived. Sheets and pillow cases were made. Beds were put up in the dorms. An apartment was remodeled and painted for our teacher, Brother Runga, and his family.

The leaders planned the Bible school dedication and a ribbon-cutting ceremony. Brother John Leaman and his wife, the Freemans, and the Hughes were our special guests. Brother Hughes was the Regional Field Supervisor of Africa, replacing Brother Freeman.

Brother Leaman was a very good friend of my husband. Often we visited him and his wife while on deputation and had been in many missions conferences together. It was a pleasure to have them come to our dedication. This was truly a great day. God blessed in the service. The ribbon-cutting was exciting.

The Bible school was a means of bringing the churches together. It would be the first time all nationalities were welcome at our Bible school. They would live together, study together, and travel together. The school would set a precedent for the country and our church.

Youth on Missions

Don finally felt comfortable enough to bring a large youth group from the states to our country. The international church's Youth Department contacted my husband to check the cheapest quote for the whole trip. I made many phone calls to check prices. Don booked everything. Several meetings were planned in the Johannesburg area and reservations were made at the Formula 1 Hotel near the airport.

Youth on Missions sent 30 young people. Two men from the Youth Department and their wives, the Darrell Johns, and the David Reevers, accompanied the youth. We were also honored to have the Freemans travel with us. A large bus was rented to transport everyone.

Services were held in Johannesburg. The youth prayed many of our young people through to the Holy Ghost. These services were life-changing for many of the young Americans and helped our South African youth to grow.

Don took the youth shopping at the inside market places and street vendors following the next afternoon's service. Being able to bargain with the vendors while buying different carvings and items, was one of the highlights of their trip.

Everyone got on the big bus and left for the Durban area. The Baptist Guest House was booked well in advance. When we arrived, I explained we had to share the bathrooms. The group filled the guest house which provided breakfast for everyone.

The bus driver needed a place to stay. Since all the rooms were filled, the manager made a bed for him under the stairway. He was a very good driver, keeping a sharp eye out for all of our valuables when we were off the bus. We were thankful to have had him.

The next service was held at Brother Blaire's church in the Sparks Estate area. The church was packed and the Youth in Missions group witnessed many receiving the Holy Ghost. For some it was the first time the Americans had seen so many people receive the Holy Ghost. It was an exciting and wonderful experience for our young people.

Traveling by bus the following day, we set off for the long trip to Kruger National Game Park. It is the only large game park in South Africa. Accommodations had been booked at a local prison that rented accommodations to tourists. Because it was a prison, they had armed guards, making it one of the safest places to stay. The lodging came highly recommended and the price was right. A night's stay and two meals cost less than $10 per person. The men and boys stayed in one dorm. The women and girls stayed in chalets.

Arrival at the prison was well after dark since the old bus did not make good time. The wardens were friendly, helping everyone get situated for the night. The evening meal consisted of barbeque, cooked by the wardens, two sides, and an African dessert. This was a new experience for our young visitors which they enjoyed. A short devotion followed dinner.

Before going to our chalets for the night, one of the girls told my husband she heard a lion. This made everyone stop and listen. All the girls became afraid. One of the wardens told us it was a donkey braying. The girl was from the city and had never heard that sound. Everyone had a good laugh and departed to our rooms.

An American-style breakfast was served the next morning. After breakfast, one of the girls said she wanted to call her Dad to tell him she had spent the night at a prison. After he heard her story, he laughed. The last thing he said before ending their conversation was, "Remember what I told you before you left for Africa? Don't get yourself put in prison."

The Kruger National Park entrance was a couple of hours away. Everyone was looking forward to this new experience.

The trailblazer had booked rooms at the Satara campsite which was located in the middle of the park. As we drove through the park we saw different campsites along the way.

On our way to Satara, we stopped for lunch at one of the campsites where we had our meal and quickly returned to the bus. Some time later the bus arrived at our camp. Everybody registered and found their rooms.

Late that afternoon, we loaded the bus for a special drive through the park. The youth saw more animals in one evening than they would ever see. Most animals went to the watering holes at dusk. Following our exciting drive, we returned to the camp.

The evening meal was served in the camp's dining room, and everyone thoroughly enjoyed the food. After devotion, we went to our different chalets to sleep.

Everyone was up early for the morning drive before breakfast. Lots of opportunities to take pictures of the animals made it a fun time.

Don had the driver take the nearest exit to the main road towards Johannesburg. Breakfast was at a privately-owned game farm. It had guest houses, a restaurant, and a small curio shop. Several small South African game were kept on their land and many were very tame. The youth had fun approaching and petting the different animals.

After breakfast, a young impala poked his nose into the window opening of the dining room. One of the girls removed a twenty-dollar bill from her purse and held it out to the impala. Half of it disappeared in a flash before she could get it away from him. At first she was upset about losing her money but she finally laughed about it, while we joined in the laughter.

Once again, we loaded everyone on the bus and were on our way to the Johannesburg area. The Lord blessed the services with the Youth on Missions.

The last night in Johannesburg, we took our busload to the Carnivore Restaurant at the edge of the city. There were only two such restaurants in the world and considered Africa's greatest eating experience, one in South Africa and one in Kenya. Nightly they served five kinds of game meat. Beef, lamb, and pork were available for those who did not want to try the game. It was an all-you-can-eat meats cooked on an open fire and served on swords. After the young people pooled their money, they invited the bus driver to join them. He had never been in a large restaurant and nor had seen so much food. It was probably one of the greatest highlights of his life. The youth really enjoyed this restaurant and it was a one-of-a-kind experience.

This was the last chance to be with the youth because they were flying back to the states. Four of the youth had come to stay longer for a special project to build a church in a village in Bophuthatawana.

An Outstanding Foursome

Sister Nix picked up the four Americans, two young girls and two young boys, from our home to travel to the old Moffat Mission, where we would all stay.

Making hand-made cement blocks for a church building was to be their mission. Daily they worked tirelessly as a team. Don kept an eye on the supplies to make sure they had enough. Services were held almost every evening in the villages. The youth adapted well to their new schedule and did an outstanding job.

One night during our service, the generator went off which left us with no lights. Several times the men tried to get it to work but to no avail. That night, one of the young men preached for the first time without his notes.

When the little church was completed, the four young people left a very happy pastor and saints with a lasting impact on the village.

Arrangements had been made to travel to the Cape area for services with the youth. It was cheaper to take them by bus than two cars. Early that morning, we arrived at the bus terminal so the youth could get good seats for the long trip to Cape Town. The front seats were their choice next to the big plate glass windows. Brother and Sister Dan and my husband and I took the seats right behind them. All went well until we were stopped by the police.

Police told our driver he must go around the area because there were problems on the main road. Men were stopping cars and buses while taking people's valuables.

The bus driver set out on the back roads. After awhile there were only dirt roads. He kept driving. Not wanting to alarm our young guests, we prayed silently. It took hours to go the back way. Either the driver knew the roads or the Lord guided him. The bus bounced over ruts and rocks yet the driver continued on his way. About daybreak, the driver came to the main road. Thank the Lord we safely made it to Cape Town.

Once again, the Lord blessed us with an outpouring of His Spirit in the services. Hearts were hungry for God and ready to receive Him. After the services in Cape Town, it was time for the youth to return to the states.

Visit by Denise

Not long after the Youth in Missions left, my niece, Denise Uecker, came to visit and stayed two months. She arrived in time for the General Conference in Cape Town. Brother Mark Christian was to be our special speaker. Don drove to Cape Town, stopping in the little town of Kimberly for service where he taught a Bible study. Everyone enjoyed the service. The next day we set off to Cape Town where we had a wonderful conference.

A few days before Christmas, Don booked a bus to take us from Cape Town to Namibia, an all-night trip. The next morning we arrived in the capital city, Windhoek. It was nice to visit our friends, the Louws, and their children, Jonathan and Bethany, for the holidays. The girls had a great time together. Brother Louw scheduled special services in their new church where my husband preached and four people received the Holy Ghost.

After New Year's Day, we returned to the Bible school. Soon after our return, Sister Nix called to ask us to go with her to visit Zimbabwe for special services. Don, Denise, and I set off for Mafeking where we accompanied Sister Nix to Bulawayo, a town in Zimbabwe. My husband preached for one of the Black pastors and the church was packed. There were no extra seats. People sat wherever they could find a space, some two to a chair. Children sat on the platform. The altar area was filled. Several people were filled with the Holy Ghost during that remarkable service.

Leaving Bulawayo, Sister Dorothy Edwards traveled with us in Sister Nix's very small crowded car to Victoria Falls. Victoria Falls borders Zambia and Zimbabwe and is roughly twice the height of North America's Niagara Falls. It is the world's largest sheet of falling water.

Don and I had visited it many times from the Zambian side. We stayed at a guest house on the Zimbabwe side.

On our return trip to Bulawayo, we stopped at the Hwange Game Park for two nights where Denise saw many different game and then headed to Sister Dorothy Edwards' house.

Arrival in Bulawayo was later than expected, but thankfully, we had time to rest before the Sunday service. Don preached Sunday morning and God moved in a mighty way. One of our pastors brought a visitor to the service. The man had planned to commit suicide but in that service God touched him. Afterwards, he went home to burn all his witchcraft paraphernalia. God marvelously filled him with the Holy Ghost that night, and he became a new man.

On Monday morning, we returned to Mafeking where we spent the night. The next morning Don and I left for South Africa. Denise decided to stay a few days with Sister Nix before returning to the states. She learned to drive on the other side of the road and was able to visit five countries during her two-month visit. It had been a trip of a lifetime for her.

Special Time with Grandsons

While we were in Namibia for Christmas, the Lord had paved the way for Keith, our son, and his wife, Beth, and sons, Jordan and Benjamin, to fill in as furlough replacements for our friends the Louws.

My husband and I met them at the airport to get them settled into the nice apartment the Louws had found for them. It was inspiring to see Keith following in his Dad's footsteps.

Don and I had enrolled Jordan in the All Nations Christian School. How wonderful it was to spend time with our grandsons. Don took them to the Namib Desert to see the highest dunes in the world. They enjoyed climbing to the top. Their papa was a great storyteller and loved sharing many stories with them.

The six of us visited the little churches in Namibia. When we left Namibia, we flew to South Africa. We were packed and ready to say goodbye before leaving on deputation. It was always hard to leave.

The next few months were a whirlwind as we raced from state to state raising our missions budget. That summer was a very special time for our grandson, Mikey, who traveled with us for a few weeks. Papa and Mikey found time to fish, went on boat rides and played games. These were rare days in the life of a missionary. Soon we found ourselves homeward bound. My husband was anxious to return to South Africa as there had been many changes in the past few months.

Following our return, we were able to travel to Windhoek to see Keith and his family. They were happy and very busy in the work of God. They loved Namibia and the people.

End of Apartheid

In many areas, South Africa's government was busy setting up voting locations accessible to all. Security of the country was stepped up, helped by the Army. Other countries were on stand-by. Extra on-duty officers were scheduled for the voting days. South Africa was expecting riots and violence. Weeks and months before the election, the crime rate was higher. Almost every other week armored trucks were blown up and many people murdered.

The United Pentecostal Church International was fasting and praying all over the world for a smooth history-making voting. God was watching over all of us. Voting could not be done in one day but required several days because people had to walk quite a distance or take some type of transportation to a voting place.

At last the voting began. Newspapers and radio daily kept everyone informed. Lines in many locations were at least a mile long in the extreme African sun. It was a very slow process in the villages and rural areas. In some areas, it was reported people showed kindness to those standing in the long voting lines. Water was distributed to everyone, regardless of their nationality.

South Africans were holding their breath, afraid of what might happen. Even though they had a problem counting the votes, everyone remained calm. South Africa did not experience the uproar that had been anticipated. During the elections, there was a lull in violence for several days. The hand of the Lord was on the country and the church.

Two men, F. W. de Klerk and Nelson Mandela, were leading the way to unify South Africa. Their example of a right attitude and a right spirit was outstanding. These men did not know God like we do yet they led the country to a new beginning.

Voting was finished and votes were counted. When it was time for F. W. de Klerk to leave office, he graciously stepped down and handed the leadership to Mandela. When it was time for Mandela to cross the threshold where no African had ever been, he took F. W. de Klerk by the arm and the two men walked together. The European radio announcer's voice cracked with emotion as he reported people were crying and dancing with joy in the streets.

Not long after this momentous day, a newsman interviewed F. W. de Klerk. He asked if he and Mandela were friends. The former State President answered, "No, but we have an excellent working relationship." What an attitude. We, the church, could do no less. Mandela had worked with his predecessor de Klerk to negotiate a long-awaited and hard-fought end to the apartheid state, for which both were jointly awarded the Nobel Peace Prize in 1993. An excellent working relationship was needed to bring unity and revival to South Africa.

While South Africa's first free and fair election passed off peacefully, there were sporadic incidents of violence following the elections.

Our church was making history in that land and began singing a song of victory, "The Church is Moving On." How true these words. God's glorious church was moving forward together. Problems and times of discouragement would be ahead but we knew God's grace was sufficient. We could sing as David did. "Then was our mouth filled with laughter, and our tongue with singing, then said they among the heathen (unbelievers). The Lord hath done great things for us: whereof we are glad" (in Psalms 126:2-3).

South Africa's transition from multiracial apartheid to democracy stands as one of the most significant political events of the last century. It improved the economic welfare of the White minority and the Black majority. The transition was peacefully negotiated. Though peaceful, the constitutional negotiations were far from harmonious.

The trailblazer and the committee could see the hand of God helping them work out many situations and issues, when there seemed to be no answers. God came through bringing victory and harmony. Only God can change the thinking and attitudes of people and bring about perfect peace.

In a Blink of an Eye

It was time for another Women's conference. Sister Helen Anderson, from the states, was invited to be our guest speaker and looked forward to coming to South Africa.

Bloemfontein was selected for the site of that year's conference which was located in the middle of the country, and easier for the ladies from the Cape to attend. Ladies came from all over the country. Sister Anderson blessed us with her songs and sermons. The ladies enjoyed visiting with her. Ladies ministries in the country grew and matured with many national speakers who were well respected.

Sister Anderson stayed with us a few days before leaving. Returning home, Brother Dan and his wife followed us. Enroute, Sister Anderson sat in the back seat. In awhile, we stopped for petrol and something cold to drink. Don told Sister Anderson to watch her purse as she had her window down. All at once, a man ran up to the car, reached in the window, and grabbed her purse. All her money, credit cards, and passport were in it. When she screamed, the thief ran around the corner with her purse. Brother Dan jumped out of his car and chased him. Suddenly, we heard gun shots. Don quickly got out of the car to see what happened to Brother Dan.

When my husband turned the corner, there was Brother Dan holding Sister Anderson's purse. Apparently when Brother Dan got close, the thief threw the purse. Thank the Lord the thief missed Brother Dan when he shot. Surely the angel of the Lord had been with Sister Anderson. What a miracle to retrieve her purse, and we thanked God for His protection.

Oranges for Christmas

The Bible school in Pelindaba reopened. Students began to do outreach in the area. During their outreach at the beginning of the school year, a student witnessed to a local white couple who started coming to church at the Bible school since they lived in the area. Husband and wife were baptized and filled with the Holy Ghost before Christmas.

After we arrived home from the long Christmas holiday, the husband gave his testimony. God had done a work in their lives the day before Christmas. His wife had begged him to take her to her parents for Christmas and surprise them. Things were getting better in the country and the husband felt it would be safe to take the trip.

Luggage, fresh oranges, food, and presents were packed in their pickup and off they went. It was getting dark when they passed a lone black man hitchhiking by the road. When they passed the man, the Holy Ghost spoke to this new baby Christian and said, "Stop and pick up the man."

The husband said to himself, "There is no way I can as my wife is with me It might not be safe." The young man continued driving.

God spoke to him again and said, "Turn around. Go back and pick up the man. Give him a ride."

At last he made a u-turn in the middle of the deserted road. When he turned the pickup around, his wife asked, "What are you doing?

Replying, he said, "The Lord told me to turn around and pick up the black man we passed. I am to give him a ride."

The wife became very upset and said, "There may be others in the bushes waiting for us to stop. They will storm the truck and attack us. Don't go back."

Again he said, "The Lord told me to stop."

By now they were near the black man. The young man made another u-turn and stopped alongside him. The husband asked the man, "Where are you going?" He told him the name of his village. The young man said they would give him a ride to his destination.

The hitchhiker got in the back seat. On the seat was a big box of oranges, food, and gifts to take to the wife's parents. As they rode along, the man did not talk much. The husband had been having a silent argument with the Lord for the past few kilometers. God had said to him, "You have a 50 rand note (South African currency) in the door of your truck. Give it to the man when you let him out."

Still the man silently argued, "God, you had me stop and give him a ride. Now you want me to give him my 50 rand note that I keep for an emergency?"

After a couple of hours they came near the man's village. As they slowed down to let him out, the wife said to their passenger, "You can take the oranges and food to your family for Christmas." The husband put his hand into the driver's door, took out the 50 rand note, and gave it to the man.

When the man got out of the pickup, he fell to his knees thanking them while saying, "Now I know there is a God that answers prayer. When you passed me I said, If there is a God, let that white man turn around and give me a ride to my village. Have him give me something to take to my family for Christmas." By now the man was weeping. Being out of work, he had no money to take anything to his family. The couple went on their way rejoicing that they had heard the voice of the Lord when He spoke to them; and they had obeyed. God taught that young couple a valuable lesson.

This testimony was good for our students. They would need to hear the voice of the Lord and care for others. If a baby Christian could do it, they could.

A Dream Comes True

Dick Ikerd, Don's brother, flew from California for a visit. Several times my husband had tried to get him to visit Africa. He arrived just in time to attend Sister Nix's new church dedication in Mafeking. All our South African churches were invited to this three-day special event. The three of us stayed at an old Mafeking Catholic mission. The Mafeking church was the first United Pentecostal church built in the country of Bophuthatawana. God mightily blessed this meeting.

Don took his brother to many places. They flew to Namibia to visit Keith and his family. Keith loaded his Dad, uncle, his wife and boys in his old Range Rover that had no air conditioning, seat belts nor car seats. He took them to Etosha National Park in Namibia. Afterwards, they traveled for services in Swakopmund and Walvis Bay. What a fascinating trip for Dick.

The brothers went sightseeing in Windhoek. The following weekend, they paid a visit to Gobabis. This town is known as "little Texas" due to it being the cattle area of the country.

Gobabis was a new area in need of a church. Dick felt led of the Lord to buy the land for this church in memory of his late wife. A few years later Brother Louw built a church on the land which is still in use today.

The next day, my husband and Dick flew back to Johannesburg. After a couple days at home, we drove to Kruger National Park. This was the first national park of South Africa. We stayed at a privately-owned cottage outside the park for a couple of days. Dick and Don had a great time and saw the big five animals: African lion, African elephant, Cape buffalo, African leopard, and White/Black rhinoceros. The brothers laughed and talked as we drove through the park. Because we had to be out of the park by sunset, we could only drive so far each day.

On our way home we stopped for lunch in the lovely little town of Nelspruit. Dick was able to buy several souvenirs from sidewalk vendors. What a wonderful visit we had with his brother. The trip was a dream come true.

A Soldier Goes Home

After Dick left, we were busy traveling and returned to the Bible school in Pelindaba. One morning Sister Nix called to tell me she had had a strange dream. Again the following day, she called to say she felt God was telling her something. That next weekend we were having special services in downtown Johannesburg and had asked Sister Nix to stay, but she was anxious to return home.

Sister Nix and her AIM worker started for her home in Mafeking. Along the way, a terrible auto accident threw Sister Nix from the car and she was severely hurt. She was taken to a small local hospital and later airlifted to Morningside Hospital in Johannesburg.

Word of the accident was received on our cell phone during a church service. My husband had the congregation stand and pray for her. Immediately we left to go to the hospital.

Don called headquarters and Brother Bill Nix, the cousin of Sister Nix, to notify them of the accident. Sister Nix had never married and had no siblings. Two helicopters were used to fly us to the hospital. When we arrived at the hospital, Sister Nix was in a coma. For three weeks, we stayed in a nearby hotel to be close to her. I owed it to my friend to be with her. Sister Nix never regained consciousness and passed away exactly three weeks after her accident.

Sister Nix's funeral was held at her church in Mafeking. Afterwards, her body was flown home to the states for a going-home service in Houston, Texas.

We lost a tremendous missionary. Sister Nix had done a wonderful work in opening the new work in Bophuthatawana and had spent many years of labor in Zimbabwe.

First Multiracial Bible School Graduation

The trailblazer and I kept the road ablaze between Pelindaba and Mafeking for four months following Sister Nix's funeral. The following month was the SABI's first graduation. It was to be held during our General Conference in Durban.

There was great excitement at the school. Much planning went into the formal banquet for the first graduating class. A rented hall was decorated with the school colors; a delicious meal of international cuisine was served. Board members and their wives were invited. Special speeches were made in honor of the top students and teachers. This landmark banquet would be remembered for many years.

The highlight of the conference was the first graduation, with Brother Hughes our guest speaker. You could feel the presence of God in a powerful way. A precedent had been set in our land as SABI became a pacesetter for many other Bible schools. The graduating young men were like the Hebrew children in the book of Daniel. They had been equipped in knowledge of the Word of God. The graduating students accomplished what had not been possible in South Africa for almost 50 years. Strong bonds had developed as they worked, studied, fasted, and prayed together. Some of these friendships would last a lifetime.

Victory Fires

Twenty-three pastors, ministers, and laymen from the United States paid their way to hold an A Team Crusade throughout South Africa. Don grouped the A Team with our board members, leaders and some of the Bible school students.

Don had me accompany one team going to the Free State area in South Africa. The team was excited as it traveled through the Kalihari

Desert seeing the need for revival. God moved mightily pouring out His spirit on hungry souls everywhere. After preaching in many areas, the A Team left revival fires burning.

The teams returned to Johannesburg after the schedule of services. Everyone was excited to see the reports of each team. Over 300 had been filled with the Holy Ghost giving us a grand total of over 650 being filled with the Spirit in the last two years.

Brother and Sister Jerry Richardson were always a great blessing to these meetings. We thanked God for sending the men who had a great burden for Africa and for lost souls.

Bophuthatswana's Transition

Keith and Beth came to Mafeking on an AIM assignment just before Easter to stay for one year. For the first time in our lives, we were only three and one-half hours away from our son and his family. Jordan, their oldest, was enrolled in Kingsway Christian School, where he was top of his class. Benjamin was not yet in school but loved visiting the crocodile farm as often as he could. He had a great love for animals - their dog named Wrinkles being his favorite.

What a blessing Keith and his wife were to the work in Bophuthatawana and especially the church in Mafeking after the death of Sister Nix. The government decided to put the little country of Bophuthatawana into South Africa allowing that district to become a part of the South African church, adding six licensed ministers. What a tremendous blessing Brother and Sister Jerry Richardson were during this process. Keith was able to help them with this transition.

Special Request

Our board members wanted to invite the first non-White speaker for the General Conference. Don asked Brother Scism to recommend a special speaker, and he recommended a California pastor, Brother Moses Hightower. He definitely was a real American Black.

The conference was held in December, which was our summer. While the minister preached on an extremely hot summer day, our interpreter fainted. Never missing a beat, the brethren jumped onto the platform, dragged the interpreter to the edge and lowered him to the floor. Another brother leaped to the platform and started interpreting.

In one of his sermons he spoke on tithing. It was an outstanding message and well received. He let them know to rob God was worse than robbing Wells Fargo (bank).

The people were truly blessed by this minister's anointed preaching. His messages left an impact on the church. That conference was another great landmark for the South African church.

50-Year Celebration

The country was celebrating 50 years of the South African church. The board invited Brother and Sister Freeman to that year's General Conference. Services were to be held in Pretoria honoring their years of service. They had arrived 50 years before on a boat with their five children.

Sister Freeman contacted my husband to say they would love to come once more to South Africa. When she informed my husband Brother Freeman was not doing well and they would need to bring assistance with them, he told her, "Bring him and come because we have a large rented house with plenty of room."

The Bible school had just been moved to Pretoria. School was out for the long school break. Don made arrangements for special services in nearby areas while the Freemans were with us.

Brother Freeman was in a wheelchair when he arrived but able to stand and take a few steps with help. Extra assistants flew with them and their daughter, Sandra. A single young lady and a registered nurse, who had known the Freemans for years, came to help care for Brother Freeman.

Mornings were hard on him. On Sunday the Freemans were to speak in the Black areas. Sister Freeman and the two ladies went on ahead. Don, Sandra, and I brought Brother Freeman a little later. On the way, he and my husband talked about the old days in South Africa remembering many areas and places we passed. He was happy to return to some of the areas in which he had preached so many times making it a great visit with pastors and saints.

Two weeks later, Sister Freeman took her husband to the General Conference's special service. When she wheeled him down an aisle between the two lines of preachers, it was a very emotional time for all. The Freeman's special service was beautiful and touching. The church of South Africa gave honor to the ones who came to their country first bringing this great message of truth. Many speeches were given in their honor and God blessed that day in a special way.

Thankfully, Brother Freeman was able to enjoy the special service in his honor. Afterwards, we took him home and Sister Freeman put him to bed. It was time for them to return to the states, after resting a few days.

Brother Freeman was called home to be with the Lord not too long after his trip to South Africa. It was a real privilege to give honor to a great soldier of the cross. He opened the door to many African countries. In Leviticus, Moses told us to respect the old man (Leviticus 19:32). In the New Testament, Paul gave us these instructions: "Let the elders that rule well be counted worthy of double honour, especially they who labour in the word and doctrine" (I Timothy 5:17). Brother Freeman labored for many years teaching the Word of God and taught the true doctrine of full salvation.

Adapting to the New South Africa

South Africa was growing and moving forward. Changes could be seen and felt in the churches throughout the country. The Jannie Smith family was a wonderful example to all their colleagues and willing to make changes.

The Smiths moved from Vanderbijlpark, an all-White area, to Klerksdorp to reopen a Colored church. Legally, they would not have been allowed to move into a Colored area under apartheid. Their family moved into the old church and set up housekeeping with dorm-type beds in the open-concept auditorium while Brother Smith remodeled the old parsonage. Upon completion of the parsonage, he moved his family into it, and then began remodeling the church.

Work was finally finished on the church and parsonage. God has blessed the Smith family and they are still there today.

Last Deputation

It was not long before we would go on deputation. Don was busy with all the last-minute things. His goal for this deputation was to finish raising funds for a permanent Bible school building in South Africa. He had seen the Kenyan Bible school become a reality and had built a Bible school building in Zambia. At last, the day rolled around and we found ourselves airborne, never realizing what lay ahead.

Don was not stressed about leaving for deputation because the Karl Smith family was to arrive in September. He felt the Bible school would be in good hands while he was gone.

Deputation started by making our way west visiting churches and our families. While we were on deputation, my husband was in and out of the hospital, eventually going on medical leave for a few months. Don's health did not allow him to finish, as his old body was worn out. Return tickets to South Africa were changed three times and were never used. Don finally realized he was not able to return and had to accept God's time and His plan for our future. At that time, Don made one last request of the Lord, "Let me open one more brand new church."

Return to Prescott

Brother Pence, an Arizona District Board member from Prescott Valley, had asked my husband several times over the years to come back to the old town of Prescott and start a new work when he was ready to return to the states.

Prescott needed a church since Brother Pence had moved the old Prescott church out to Prescott Valley, a new suburb, where most of his congregation lived. Prescott's climate was very nice as the high altitude kept the summer from being very hot. Winters were mild, making it an ideal location for many retired people.

A few months later, my husband called Brother Pence to let him know we were now ready to come to Prescott as his health would not permit him to return to South Africa. Brother Pence reluctantly told Don a new pastor had been approved by the Arizona District Board and had already moved to Prescott to open a new church.

When my husband finished the phone call and told me his conversation, I cried and cried. I had told the Lord there was no place I would want to go but back to Prescott. Daily we asked God's guidance for our future. During this time we stayed near our daughter, Kelli, and her son, and were able to see them almost every day. It was nice to be close to them for the first time.

Keith, Beth, and their boys settled in Alaska which was a lovely place to raise their sons. While they were there, God blessed them with a daughter, Aubrey. How delighted we were to have a granddaughter. They loved Alaska and enjoyed working in the church but we were so far away from them. Yet God's ways are not our ways. He knows best.

Don never dreamed he would not be able to return to South Africa. When we left, we never said a final goodbye because we assumed we would return after raising money for our mission budget and the new multiracial Bible School of South Africa. He felt the Bible school was the answer to bring unity to the country.

About mid-December, Don received a phone call from Brother Pence, asking him if he was still interested in Prescott. My husband told Brother Pence we were. Brother Pence had heard the man who had gone to Prescott to open the church was moving back East to take an established church. He wanted to check it out and get back to my husband.

Brother Pence invited us to their annual Christmas banquet the following week. When we got there, we learned the minister was leaving Prescott. Don applied to the District Board for permission to open a new church in Prescott and was approved.

Bags were packed and we moved to Prescott within one month. An old church building was found where we could rent a large room for service.

First Sunday service we had seven in attendance A few weeks later we had 25. Now we needed more room. Soon we were able to rent the old church parsonage, using two bedrooms for Sunday School. Again, we outgrew that and rented the main church building. Later, we found a building and the church continued to grow.

The Trailblazer Goes Home

After a serious heart problem and cancer, Don asked Brother Phelps to become the pastor and my husband assisted him. God gave my husband another year. He blazed his last trail the morning of January 25, 2008. All he had ever worked for was to hear the Lord say, "Well done thou good and faithful servant..." (Mathew 25:21). He could say, "I have fought a good fight, I have finished my course, I have kept the faith:" (II Timothy 4:7).

Epilogue

At the writing of this book, I am under an AIM appointment to the country of Namibia where I am working with my son, Keith, and his wife, Beth, who are the UPC missionaries in that country. Kelli and her family are in Arizona, which is home to them.

Our friends, the John Harris family, are now in Arlington, Texas where he is the bishop and co-pastor with his son, Jonathan.

Brother and Sister Rivers, now retired, live in San Antonio, Texas, still working for the Lord.

Brother and Sister Melvin Thacker led the church of Zambia after our departure to South Africa. They poured their hearts into the Bible school which helped the Zambian church move forward. Today they are in full-time ministry, pastoring the Apostolic Gospel Church of River Falls, Wisconsin.

The Louie Louws continue to work in foreign missions.

Brother and Sister Gary Abernathy continue foreign missions from South Africa to Malawi. Today they are still based in Zambia. They have been developing pastors and leaders, bringing the country to where it is today.

The Karl Smith family is now pastoring in Louisiana after working several years in South Africa following our return to the United States.

My husband's brother, Dick, passed away. His widow, Dot, has remarried to Roy Beams and they live in Lodi, CA where we have worked on this book for the past few months.

I was privileged to see Brother Lumina and his son on my last visit to Zambia for the Nationalization service. Chamuka is now a lawyer in Zambia.

Brother and Sister Dan Ragavaloo reside in Parlock (Durban area) South Africa.

Sister Clive Antonio is still very faithful in the work of God.

The Jannie Smith family is still living in Klerksdorp, South Africa where he pastors the church. At this writing, he is the Superintendent of the church of South Africa.

Brother Coetzee and his wife now pastor the church in Pretoria, South Africa.

Retired missionaries, Sister Carol Rash and Sister Bobbye Wendell are still very faithful in the work of God. Sister Wendell still travels preaching around the country.

The following people have gone on to their reward: Sister Helen Anderson, Brother Clive Antonio, Brother Murrell Ewing, Brother and Sister E. L. Freeman, Dick Ikerd, Donald Ikerd, Brother Edwin Judd, Sister Lumina, Brother and Sister Mokheti, Sister Wilma Nix, Brother Daryl Rash, Brother and Sister Sonkoni, and Brother and Sister Nathaniel Urshan

Acknowledgements

When I started on the book, I had no idea what hard work it would entail nor how many people it would take to get the book written. I have been blessed with a wonderful team of people who have shared experiences and have given me words of encouragement.

A special thank you goes to Dot Ikerd Beams, my sister-in-law and friend, who is the co-author of the book. She was able to read all my scribbling and misspelled words and put them into a book. What an answer to prayer you have been as you guided the book from start to finish.

Many thanks to my proofreader, Sister Margie Hoyle, who lovingly put in many long hours. What a blessing you have been.

My son, Keith, and daughter, Kelli, have been such an encouragement, providing input, and recalling many incidences as we blazed this trail together. Thank you, Kelli, for writing the Bag Lady story.

A special thanks to my cheerleaders, Fern, my sister, and her husband, Dennis Uecker.

Denise Christian, my niece, has been an invaluable help with many details and emails.

Many thanks to my graphic designer, Josh Rivas.

Tara Phelps, you did an outstanding job gathering all the photos.

Dennis B. Uecker, you were a lifesaver coming to our aid during our computer digital problem.

Special Gratitude

Special thanks to the families of William Cupples and John Harris who pioneered the Kenyan church. Kenya is blessed with good national leaders. The Jim Crumpackers have labored to bring the church where it is today.

The promise given to my husband and I in 1980 was fulfilled thirty-three years later when I was privileged to attend the Zambia Nationalization service. "Fear not, O land; be glad and rejoice: for the Lord will do great things." (Joel 2:21) A big thank you goes to all the Zambian missionaries. A special thanks goes to Brother and Sister Gary Abernathy for bringing the church of Zambia to where it is today. May the Lord bless the Zambian National Board and use them to go forward in revival.

My husband was never able to return to South Africa to tell how much he appreciated the first Executive Board that tirelessly traveled and helped him blending the races and uniting the church in South Africa. Countless thanks goes to these special men: Brother Jannie Smith, Brother Dan Ragavaloo, Brother Clive Antonio, and Brother Elias Mokheti.

Much gratitude goes to the new board of South Africa, The baton has now been passed to you. What a great responsibility you have to get the church of South Africa to the Promise Land just like Joshua of old, when Moses passed the leadership to him. You must lead the way.

I wish to personally thank the following people for their contributions to my inspiration, knowledge, and other help in creating this book: Brother and Sister J. P. Hughes, Brother Jerry Richardson, Sister Carol Rash, and Sister Lesley Kelley.

A big thank you goes to all who have touched the book in any way.

Comments

We first met the Ikerds when they came as fellow missionaries to the beautiful country of Kenya. Our families formed a close friendship. Their children, Keith and Kelli, were near in age to our children and they all loved to play together. We spent great times with them on vacation, eating at each other's houses, playing games, and just visiting with each other.

I spent three years working closely with Don in Kenya and Ethiopia in the Kingdom of God. He was a faithful, hard working man of God who had great humor. He cheered us many times with his stories from deputation and travels in the bush. Don Ikerd was an outstanding speaker, good organizer, and was loved by all who knew him. With him stood, Sharon, his faithful wife working for the Lord. She continues her Work for the Kingdom in a foreign field.

Their son, Keith, is a missionary in Africa doing a great job, along with his wife, Beth. The legacy of Don Ikerd lives on as a good example and encouragement to all of us because his top priority and main goal in life was to promote God's Kingdom on this earth. We rejoice to think that now he is enjoying his eternal reward.

Charles Harris
Superintendent and pioneer in Africa
Bible School Founder and President

We met the Donald Ikerd family in February of 1978. The Donald Rivers family soon discovered they were servants, not self-serving, rather serving others.

At one o'clock in the morning of February 3, 1978, the Rivers arrived in Nairobi airport exhausted from their 30-plus hour flight. They arrived at the church compound in Nairobi to discover that their belongings had been carefully placed into the former home of the Ikerd's. The beds were made and ready for the exhausted travelers. They snuggled in their beds after 3 am.

Meanwhile, the Ikerd's had quietly moved to rooms in the Bible school. In the months to follow, we were to see a model missionary family serve the Kenyans in their humble way. They had abandoned the comforts of America to teach the Kenyan people how to live an Apostolic lifestyle.

If you were to look for a flamboyant ministry, you would not find it. The Ikerd's served in practical ways of honesty, simplicity and truth. Donald Ikerd, in his quiet way, would persevere to establish truth in the hearts of honest Kenyan people. Thus, Kenya was to grow and become a model of Christian Apostolic Faith.

During our stay in Kenya, we were to observe, on a daily basis, Donald Ikerd quietly teaching the Kenyans with humor and his natural talent. He approached the Kenyans on a level they could receive. Donald Ikerd would teach and preach to the men and Sharon Ikerd would passionately preach to a hungry audience of women. The alters would rapidly fill with receptive hearts to the truth. The Ikerd's were a couple totally dedicated to the cause of Jesus Christ.

Miracles of healing and deliverance were to occur on a regular basis as a tribute to their sacrifice and service.

Our children received love and affection from the Ikerd family and learned to love and respect their sacrifice. To this day, they are quick to sing their praise and affection for the Ikerd's from their experience as young children growing up in Kenya

Donald Rivers
Missionary to Africa

The Trailblazer is Sharon Ikerd's first book. She is now in Namibia Africa on an Associates in Missions (AIM) project. Her sister-in-law, Dot Beams, is the co-author of this book. Graduating with a B.S. in Theology from the Apostolic Bible Institute, she was active in women's ministries for many years. She is currently active in Widows Fellowship. Dot has authored two stories in Chicken Soup for the Soul for Twins and More, one story in Chicken Soup for the Soul Amazing Miracles, and several stories in An Oasis Moment. She lives in California with her husband.

Made in the USA
San Bernardino, CA
26 September 2017